Grose Ltd.
Northampton

CW00684363

Specialists in MOTOR COACHWORK

LUXURIOUS "GROSE" BODIES
THE ACME OF FINISH AND STYLE

CABRIOLET-COUPÉS   LIMOUSINES

LANDAULETTES   SALOONS

OPEN BODIES   CABRIOLETS

SPORTING AND ALL-WEATHER BODIES

Under existing circumstances, we regret our inability to state definite prices for the different types of bodies presented in this list.   But we shall be most pleased, upon receipt of enquiry (with blue-print of chassis if possible), to give detailed specification and quotation to hold good for a stated period.

Telegrams—"Case, Northampton."
Telephone No. 111.

MEMORANDUM FROM

GROSE LTD.

MANUFACTURERS OF

The "GROSE" Original Non-Skidding and Puncture-Proof
Tread for Motor Cars and Motor Cycles.

PIKE LANE, MAREFAIR,

Northampton,

Joseph Grose

AND THE MOTOR CAR

A True Pioneer

Joseph George Grose (1861-1939)

JOSEPH GROSE
AND THE MOTOR CAR

A True Pioneer

Alan Burman

Phillimore

1998

Published by
PHILLIMORE & CO. LTD.
Shopwyke Manor Barn, Chichester, West Sussex

© Alan Burman, 1998

ISBN 1 86077 090 8

Printed and bound in Great Britain by
BIDDLES LTD.
Guildford, Surrey

Contents

List of Illustrations

Frontispiece: Joseph George Grose (1861-1939)

Acknowledgements and Introduction

It is now close on forty years since I first became interested in the Joseph Grose saga. My interest in local history and my obsession with motor vehicles fused and I realised that here, on my doorstep, was a significant figure in the early days of motoring. My first researches were stumbling; it was merely a hobby. It began to get serious when I realised that much historic material was being lost in the developments that were going on within Grose Ltd. At one stage a mass of photographs was about to be dispersed and I managed to obtain permission to take photographic copies of them. Some of the originals survived, many did not and have since disappeared. The final straw came when the firm moved from Marefair to Queen's Park. Shuffling through the debris that littered the now empty old garage I came across many shattered glass plates, old photographic negatives of Grose coachwork. These I saved, fitting the fragments together to make contact prints, and retouching out the joins. I was jolted awake to the urgency of the situation. If it was not recorded soon, the history of Grose coachwork would be lost. I was irrevocably locked into the task that has resulted in this volume.

Since I started accumulating the information that led eventually to the conception of this book, I have spoken to so many enthusiasts and experts that it is impossible to mention them all or, indeed, to remember who told me what! Casual conversations at vintage car meetings often elicited odd snippets of information that, pasted into the general picture, added vital highlights to the story.

Other authors, working on marque histories, fed me morsels picked up when their lines of research crossed mine, and an appeal in the Northampton newspaper brought forth many ex-employees who delighted in recalling the heyday of their craft. To all these people go my sincere thanks.

There were others, of course, who were the core of my support: John Grose whose desire to see his grandfather's contribution to motoring history preserved in print equalled my own and whose enthusiasm and encouragement kept the fires burning, James Fack and his fellow archivists of the Sunbeam Talbot Darracq register who came up with amazingly detailed data, Roger Warwick whose knowledge of Northamptonshire bus services is encyclopedic, and the staff of the Northamptonshire Libraries Local Studies unit who fetched and carried innumerable hefty volumes during my search with great good humour. Particularly, I would mention the happy folk who staff the National Motor Museum archive at Beaulieu. During my many visits, each short and frantic because I live so far away, they have pulled out all the stops to achieve the most in the shortest time, and have done it cheerfully.

Since no data, drawings, or ledgers relating to Grose coachwork survive, this book has been put together by patching together information from innumerable sources. Of course, it is inevitable that, once the book is in print, hitherto undiscovered material will emerge. This I can do nothing about. All the information gathered here has received written contemporary corroboration or is confirmed from at least two separate sources. Errors, should there be any, I accept as my own.

Finally, and any author of a motoring history will know what I mean, I acknowledge my wife Beryl's resigned acceptance of many lonely hours and an untended garden during the gestation of my 'baby'!

Foreword

The 'Motor Car'–two words that today we accept without thought.

The contribution the motor car has made to our modern day world equals, if not surpasses, that of all other inventions that have become an accepted part of 20th-century life.

The steps that civilisation has taken during the past 100 years are almost frightening– in science, travel, medicine, electronics, engineering, the list is endless. The twin foundation stones of it all are, without doubt, the invention of electricity and the internal combustion engine. Almost everything that we accept today as common place depends in some measure on one or other of these things.

From an engineering point of view the motor car, as opposed to its propulsion unit, grew from the bicycle and the pioneers of bicycling became the entrepreneurs of automobilism.

Joseph Grose, my grandfather, was one of the élite band of men who laid the foundations of the great world-wide industry that we see today. This book is the story of one of those special men who had the foresight, the courage, and the tenacity to overcome the many obstacles which were placed before motoring trail-blazers. He and his contemporaries brought into being the machine which we now take for granted, which jumps to life at the touch of a button, shows us 'the other side of the hill' and, in short, widens our horizons in innumerable ways.

This is a tribute both to my forebear, just one of those pioneers to whom we owe so much and, I add, to Alan Burman, without whose journalistic skills and dedication to motoring this story would not have been brought to light.

JOHN GROSE
1 October 1998

One

Pioneer Days

It was Saturday, 24 April 1897, a busy market day in Northampton. The town was thronged, women were shopping for the weekend, menfolk were hurrying about their business, and, as always, there were the usual knots of tradesmen or idlers grouped here and there. Suddenly a strange and unfamiliar sound intruded above the usual clatter of horseshoes and iron-clad wheels on granite setts, the frantic chuff of an internal combustion engine. The motor-car had arrived!

The vehicle that came into view was a three-wheeled device with one wheel at the back, motorcycle style, and two at the front between which was a passenger seat. Piloting the tricycle was Mr. Joseph Grose, who owned a bicycle business at the lower end of Gold Street, and in the 'suicide seat' was Mr. H. 'Doc' Green, an engineer so nick-named for his wizardry in restoring life to ailing industrial gas engines.

After a brief run into Marefair the intrepid pair turned to take a run at the long incline of Gold Street. Their progress created chaos. Horses skipped and skittered, shops emptied of customers, errand boys ran alongside or raced on their delivery bikes, and startled ladies backed against the walls.

All went well for Grose and Green until they reached the area in front of All Saints' Church. Here the granite setts gave way to wooden blocks, set in tar to form the road surface and intended to reduce traffic noise around the church and the courthouse. These blocks, saturated with rain and the ordure of countless horses, were extremely slippery. The Motette promptly spun, pirouetting gracefully before coming to an undignified halt. Thus ended the first outing of the first motor vehicle in Northampton.

To chart the progress of motoring pioneer Joseph Grose we must go back to his birth in February 1861. His father, also Joseph, was the keeper of the tollgate on the Bedford road near the Great Houghton Lane. A native of Napton, in Warwickshire, Joseph senior married a Braunston girl, Mary Pebody, nine years his senior, who had already given him four children,

1 *Joseph Grose and 'Doc' Green aboard the Coventry Motette for their first outing, 1897*

1

2   *Grose with the racing 'ordinary' that he built himself*

William Mark Anthony aged 11, Phillip aged eight, Samuel aged six, and Catherine Anne aged four, by the time the new son arrived on 12 January 1861.

The road from Northampton to Cold Brayfield, Bedfordshire, had been turnpiked in the late 1820s, and the Great Houghton tollgate was set up in 1826-7 being let out at £416 a year. In 1844 an attempt was made to raise the rent to £420 but the railways were making great inroads into turnpike income and it had to be let for £414. Three years later the rent decreased again to £370. Tollkeepers everywhere were forced to supplement their living by taking a second trade. When Joseph took on the job in 1853 he sidelined as a tailor, and thus he is listed in the records of Great Houghton church where Joseph George Grose was baptised on 3 March 1861. The Bedford Road was the last turnpike in the county to survive, operating until 1880, but Joseph and his family by then had given up Tollgate House and moved to town.

Young Joseph was only four years old when his parents moved to St James's End. There he sang with the church choir and as a youth started work as a currier, processing skins into leather, one of Northampton's staple trades. A stocky teenager, he excelled at athletics, particularly racing the high 'ordinary' bicycles of the day, commonly known as 'penny-farthings'.

At the age of 17, in 1878, he raced his machine in the One Mile Open Handicap held on the cycle track behind the *Halfway House* pub in Kingsthorpe Hollow. He was scratch man in his heat on the 210-yard mark. His brother Phillip, obviously considered a faster rider, raced in another heat from the 220-yard mark. The finals were run the following Saturday, but neither Grose was placed.

He must have been a fit man, if the stories told about him are true. It is said that he used to ride his machine out to Harpole turn where he would meet a fellow racer called Wilson. The pair would then ride to the Birmingham track, take part in a day's hard racing, and then ride back home, a round trip of some 80 miles.

Five years on and Joseph had improved enough to create a record at the Aylestone Grounds track at Leicester by covering 20 miles in 59 minutes 18 seconds. The machine that he used was an ultra-lightweight that he had built himself weighing only 19lbs. with a 52in. diameter wheel.

In June 1884 Grose raised his own record on the more difficult track at Crystal Palace. The old 'pennyfarthing' was limited by the size of the driving wheel, which could only be as large as the rider's inside leg measurement. To overcome this the Kangaroo-type machine had been invented with a smaller wheel, still between the riders legs, but geared. On such a bicycle Grose covered the 20 miles in exactly 58 minutes.

His reputation as a cycle athlete was by now national and in 1885 he paced the great racer J.H. Adams when that rider tackled the 24-hour road record. This, and the fact that he was by now building bicycles for other riders who were beating a path to his door as a result of his success, categorised him as a professional rider even though he was occupied running his own business as a currier and leather seller at 39, Richmond Road, St James's End.

On 4 April 1888 he took part in the 50-Mile Professional Championships at Aylestone Grounds, one of his last competitions, as business commitments were taking up so much of his time.

The Grose family were all doing well. Joseph had married Mary Elizabeth Stanley at St James's Church in 1886. Joseph's older brother William was trading

3 *The Kangaroo, a geared 'ordinary', on which Grose broke several records*

as a beer retailer and general shopkeeper just round the corner at 16 Ambush Street, while his mother and sister were close by at 49 Richmond Road, earning a living as dressmaker and laundress respectively. Brother Phillip was also a currier and bootmaker at 4 Adelaide Street.

It was plain to Joseph that there was money to be made in bicycles. The bicycle boom that came with the invention of the safety bicycle had created an entirely new pastime. Not only that, it had revolutionised the lives of everybody. At last the man in the street could work miles away from home, he could meet and marry a girl from many villages away, and his horizons were limitless. Joseph took a small shop at 21 St James's Road and set up as a cycle agent.

The arrival of the safety bicycle meant that for the first time women could ride, and the prospect of disappearing into the countryside alone with your lady-love made the hobby hugely popular. There were no less than 12 cycling clubs in Northampton at this time. One big drawback for the fashionable lady was that, wearing the long skirts then in vogue (and necessary to hide one's ankles from view), hems tended to drag,

4 *Joseph Grose (on second bicycle from right) with fellow competitors in the 50-mile professional championships at Aylestone Grounds, Leicester, 1888.*

5 *Joseph and wife Mary on the new safety bicycles*   **6** *Joseph Grose's first lock-up shop at St James's End*

7   *The billhead for Grose's Gold Street business*

or become entangled in, the driving chain. Grose applied his mind to this problem and, drawing on his knowledge of leather, came up with a solution. On 18 February 1892, he applied for a patent for 'a new adjustable chain and chain wheel cover and lubricator for bicycles'.

Patent number 3162, awarded on 31 December 1892, described a metal frame covered with leather, in practice usually black patent, placed over the chain and both sprockets, and laced at the bottom by means of bootlaces and hook-eyes such as used on typical field-boots. Into the top was fixed a large lubricator in which was placed a wick that touched the chain inside the case, thus allowing a smear of oil to reach each link as it passed. Weighing a mere 9 to 12 oz and guaranteed dustproof and noiseless, it sold in basic form for £1 or, with self-adjusters and slides, 25s. Manufacture started this year with a small capital.

Other bicycling specialities followed and were likewise patented; on 23 October 1894 Number 6294, 'an improvement in the method of fastening leggings and other such gear', and on 23 October 1895, Number 19901, 'improvements in or relating to apparatus for carrying articles on velocipedes and the like (tool bag and pump clip)'. Other items that drew Joseph Grose's inventive attention were 9 oz lightweight, non-rattling patent leather mudguards, the 'Diamond' leather toolbag shaped to fit within the cycle frame, and a special combined dressguard and chaincover for ladies machines.

These developments brought great success to Grose. At larger premises at 63 Gold Street he was manufacturing and selling leather requisites for the cycle trade. He also had shops in the heart of bicycle country at St Michael's Churchyard, Coventry, and at 58 Holborn Viaduct, London. He was sole local agent for Singer, Rover, Triumph, New Premier, Osmond, and New Enfield cycles as well as many others. The founders of these companies were, many of them, old friends from Joseph's bicycle racing days, notably J.K. Starley inventor of the Ariel, the first practical 'pennyfarthing' in 1875, and the first safety bicycle in 1885. On 13 June 1896, J.K. Starley & Co. became the Rover Cycle Co., Grose establishing a link with the Rover marque which has lasted until the present day.

The Gold Street premises had formerly been a theatre and concert hall. Over one hundred feet long and forty feet wide, the ground floor was used as a display area while the gallery was used as a parts store. Leather goods, tyres, etc. were stacked on the stage once trodden by famous thespians. Twenty mechanics were engaged in the workshop area.

8 *Grose's Cycle Works on the corner of Gold Street and Horseshoe Street*

As New Year dawned in 1897 Grose was already a comparatively wealthy man. He had three children, William Thomas, Katherine, and a new baby Frank James. It was a time of great excitement. It was to be Diamond Jubilee Year, celebrating Queen Victoria's 60-year reign. Perhaps more exciting for Grose, though, the previous November had seen the enactment of the Locomotives on Highways Act which had freed the motor vehicle from the need to be preceded by a walking man and had raised the speed limit to a thrilling 14 miles per hour. Grose resolved to purchase one of these new 'horseless carriages'.

Joseph Grose was plainly bitten by the motoring bug, but where he caught the bacillus is not evident. He had been involved with an extraordinary gas-powered tram that underwent trials in the early weeks of 1883. The Northampton Street Tramway Company, operating horse trams in the town, would have liked to adopt mechanical transport. Joseph Grose, together with a chartered engineer Mr. L. Moore, the owner of Vulcan Ironworks in Guildhall Road, Mr. O. Mobbs, and 'Doc' Green produced a wooden test chassis upon which was a large cylindrical tank charged with coal-gas from the town supply. A valve reduced pressure as a gas and air mixture was fed to the large single cylinder engine. This, despite its massive 12in. bore and 18in. stroke, relied greatly upon inertia stored in a giant flywheel to enable it to travel effectively between stops. Having built up the speed of this 5ft. 3in. diameter flywheel while stationary, a steel wheel on the same shaft was brought into contact with either of two leather covered wheels to give forward or reverse motion via a final chain drive.

9 *A Grose family outing in 1896 with new baby Frank on his father's front carrier*

This device underwent trials, first of all, at the tram depot, and then on a flat stretch of track at St James's End where it successfully towed one of the horse trams containing 12 people. Despite this promising test nothing more seems to have been done about the car.

One year on and Joseph Grose was again involved, but to a lesser extent, in an even stranger invention. The *Northampton Mercury* reported the trial of a manual powered tram which successfully climbed the then considerable incline of Abington Street. Unfortunately, the details in the report are somewhat sketchy, but the machine was apparently the patented design of a group of three Lincoln businessmen based on the original invention of a Mr. J.W. Graham of that city. Construction of the test car was entrusted to Northampton bicycle makers Mr. Gadsby, proprietor of the Lion Cycle Works in Bearward Street, Mr. Jasper Berry with works in Marefair and Pike Lane, and Joseph Grose who was Berry's close friend and business partner.

10   *The full touring version of the Coventry Motette, complete with awning*

The mechanism of this vehicle would appear to have been treadle-powered and connected through gears to the driving wheels. Whether all the passengers were expected to pedal or whether it was only the tramway staff is unclear but, like its predecessor, it relied greatly on stored inertia in a large flywheel. The drive incorporated a primitive two-speed gear train.

The final trigger for Grose's purchase of a motor vehicle may have come from Arthur Felton Mulliner who, a stone's-throw away from Grose's premises, was already building bodies for self-propelled vehicles. Or maybe it was from his old ex-cycle-racer friends, many of whom were dabbling in the burgeoning motorcar business.

Among these friends was Charles McRobie Turrell, who had taken part in the great Emancipation Run to Brighton aboard a Daimler, was a member of the Lawson Motor Syndicate that operated from the Motor Mills at Coventry, and was general manager of the Coventry Motor Co., which had acquired the rights to manufacture the French-designed Leon Bollee tricar under licence as the Coventry Motette. It was the third of these fast English-built three-wheelers to leave the Motor Mills that Joseph Grose purchased.

The Motette was a fast and reliable machine. The single cylinder was set low down alongside the rear wheel giving a low centre of gravity. The whole vehicle weighed only 280lbs. It had an atmospheric inlet valve and ignition was by hot platinum tube, a device by which a tube projecting from the cylinder head was heated by a petrol burner to incandescence, the mixture in the cylinder being compressed into it on the piston's upstroke and thus ignited. The price of the basic model was £150, although a more powerful version with a larger bore, built especially for hilly districts, with three speeds giving 5, 14, and 20 miles per hour and capable of climbing gradients up to 1 in 7, was available. As an accessory a Surrey awning in velvet plush with silk tasselled trim at £15 extra was also offered.

After Joseph Grose's first disastrous outing on the Saturday it was on the following Monday, 26 April, 1897, that Grose ventured on to the highway again with his new machine. As before, the progress of this fearsome machine created chaos among the horses wherever it went. Equally, the *Northampton Mercury* reported, word had got about and people seemed anxious to study the workings of this latest method of travelling. Large crowds assembled around the vehicle at every point where it stopped. All went well until one o'clock that afternoon when Grose's trike throbbed its way up Cheyne Walk and turned into Billing Road. Coming along the road happened to be Mr. John Dilley, a butcher from Bath Street, out making deliveries in his pony and trap. The animal became alarmed at this strange and noisy contraption, reared suddenly, and threw Mr. Dilley from the trap. The butcher was carried to the nearby General Infirmary for treatment of his head injuries, which turned out not to be too serious. The pony was also slightly injured and there was considerable damage to both trap and harness.

It is worth recording, in view of later rivalry over who was the first to drive a motor-car in Northampton, that that very same week Mr. Arthur Felton Mulliner ran a Daimler car in chassis form, fresh from the factory and still in its undercoat of paint, in the town. This was probably the car which became Mulliner's own, eventually known as The Owl, and still survives. A consignment of Daimler chassis had been delivered by rail to Mulliner's in November 1896 for bodies to be built at the Bridge Street works but they were not driven upon the road. The second actual owner of a car in the town was Mr. Alfred Richardson of Elysium Terrace who bought a Benz single cylinder 3½ horse power car with solid tyres about the same time as Grose.

Whatever Grose thought of his experiences with the Motette, we find him, in the *Northampton Herald* of 3 June 1897, advertising himself as 'The Sole Agent for the District of The Coventry Motor Co. (Bollie System)'. The misspelling was probably the newspaper's!

It was customary at Whitsuntide for there to be an elaborate programme of outdoor entertainment at Franklin's Gardens, in St James's End. These pleasure gardens, long established as the Melbourne Gardens until bought, renamed, and revitalised by Mr. Franklin, the owner of a premier hotel in Guildhall Road and

11 *Exhibiting at Crystal Palace, 1897*

benefactor of the Royal Theatre and Opera House, was a great magnet for locals over the holiday period. In an advertisement in the *Herald* of 3 June, alongside Zulina, the female Samson, Captain Minting, bicyclist and spiral ascensionist, and a balloon ascent and double parachute descent by Captain Spencer and Miss Alma Beaumont, the Premier Lady Aeronaut of the World, we find that there were to be 'Two Motor Cars to carry Visitors at a Nominal Charge'. In view of Grose's later involvement and organisation of similar demonstrations, it is probable that these two cars belonged to Grose and Richardson. Grose would have been too shrewd to have invited his rival Mulliner. As it happened, there is no mention of the vehicles in the subsequent, very detailed, reports of the event, so it would seem that they did not perform!

In July 1897 a company, Grose Gear Case Ltd., was floated to manufacture the leather cases and other specialities under patent. With a capital of £25,000 the directors

12 *Grose's stand at the Northampton Corn Exchange, 1898. Beyond the bicycles four cars are displayed.*

were, as well as Joseph Grose, Councillor A.E. Phipps as chairman, Alderman W. Mills and J.K. Starley. The auditors confirmed that recent profits had been made at the rate of £8,300 per annum and that orders stood on the books for 40,000 gearcases. It is also evident that Grose had already begun acquiring properties with a view to enlarging his 63 Gold Street site, as he owned seven freehold cottages and a yard in Adelaide Place at this time.

The first thrust of the new company came when it took a large stand at the National Cycle Show held at Crystal Palace later in the year.

The peregrinations of the Motette had not gone unnoticed by medical men locally. Indeed, the national motoring press was full of information for and inquiries from doctors who immediately saw how convenient it would be not to have to keep a horse ready, harness it, and put it to a carriage, to answer an urgent call, especially at night. A quick-starting motor car would be a boon. Dr. H. Stedman of Towcester

reckoned that he could never get his horse and carriage ready at his door in under three quarters of an hour. In a letter dated 8 September 1897, he wrote to Grose:

> I understand that you are the owner of the Coventry Motette which I have seen pass here. I am thinking of getting one myself if it can be relied upon to do my work, but as I know very little about them may I call upon you about 2 pm on Friday with a view to getting a little information about them from an unbiassed source.

> I trust you will pardon the liberty I am taking without an introduction, but you will doubtless readily understand my anxiety to know something about them before investing in one. My only reason for preferring this motor to any other is that it is so highly spoken of by all the dealers in motor carriages. Of course, the Daimler would no doubt suit my purpose well enough but the price is prohibitive.

Dr Stedman very soon disposed of his Motette, purchasing a Benz Ideal from Grose. After 12 months use Dr. Stedman totted up the cost of his conveyance. In the year he had travelled 7,500 miles at a total cost of £92. This included a man's wages at £1 per week, breakages, wear and tear such as three new tyres, two new chains, eight new chain wheels, petrol, lubricating oil, various alterations and repairs, and a few small (unsuccessful) experiments, but does not include depreciation, which he estimated at 20 per cent. This worked out at 3d. a mile, comparing very favourably with 6d. a mile which a horse had cost him. Like Grose, he had found the Benz bearings inadequate, but had solved the problem by fitting plain bearings to both countershaft and rear wheels. He had also moved the controlling lever to the side of the car. To improve handling and to allow the fitting of a toolbox under the front seat (it was obviously a vis-a-vis) he lengthened the vehicle by seven inches. His unsuccessful experiments chiefly referred to jacketing the carburettor with hot water so as to be able to use benzoline in winter. During the year, Dr. Stedman said, he had never at any time used a horse for his work, nor did he ever wish to do so again! He intended, he ended up saying, having a car made to his own specifications.

This small beginning had a ripple effect in the small town of Towcester. Another Towcester man who purchased a Motette from Grose was Mr. Victor Ashby, a cycle dealer who had taken over an old Baptist Chapel on the Watling Street in 1877. In 1897 he turned it into a garage, became the local agent for the Coventry Motette, developed a thriving motor car business and eventually went on to design and make the Short Ashby car.

Yet another Motette was sold to Mr. Alan Hickman who became a prolific writer to motoring papers and an enthusiastic advocate of motoring. He attended the Northampton Motor Car and Cycle Show at the Corn Exchange in February 1898 and bought the model from Grose's show stand. He left a detailed account of a ride that he made from Northampton to the South Coast soon after he acquired it. This trip, with a Mr. Thompson as passenger, began at 8.30a.m. The 41 miles to Oxford took them 3½ hours. Onwards to Salisbury they were beset with minor problems obtaining petrol, re-setting the governors, and sorting out the town/country exhaust cut-out, but they eventually arrived safely at 8p.m., in darkness, with the lamps lit. Then followed visits to Wareham, Corfe Castle, Poole, and the New Forest. Constant difficulties came, not from the car, but from appalling roads and carters asleep as their vehicles straddled the highway which, on one occasion, forced them into a ditch.

14   *On tour with the Panhard and a Daimler*

From Lewes they headed home via London. At Kingston on Thames they had great problems finding a supplier of petrol, eventually persuading a local electrical engineer to get some especially for them. Punctures plagued them at Aylesbury and the car packed up near Towcester with a charred wick. They arrived home to find a summons awaiting them for progressing at what the local policeman called 'a terrible speed' at Corfe Castle, which cost Hickman a £1 fine and £1 4s. 6d. costs. The trip, nevertheless, was hailed as a great success in the motoring press.

Grose's early experiences with the Motette had, perhaps, confirmed the forecar's drawbacks. Conversation was difficult, the passenger was vulnerable and 'first on the scene of an accident'. Late in 1897, therefore, after visiting France and being convinced of the motor car's future, he purchased a secondhand Panhard from the Great Horseless Carriage Company. With three speeds, open bevel gears, solid tyres, and lever steering, this car was used for several long-distance tours. It was quickly converted to pneumatic tyres and wheel steering. On one occasion, with Mrs. Grose and two friends, Mr. & Mrs. C. Tompkins, as passengers, he drove to Yarmouth, the 137-mile journey taking over 12 hours, stopping every eight miles to replenish the radiator

15   *The Panhard after being rebuilt in the Grose workshops in 1899*

with water. They arrived triumphantly on the seafront early in the morning to be confronted by a police officer who asked what Grose thought he was doing. Explanations that the machine was quite harmless were of no avail and he was ordered to remove it to a safe place. All the usual livery stables refused to house the car. Eventually a mews was discovered where the Panhard could be left, but only if Mr. Grose agreed to insure the building against fire and explosions! The car remained there for two days during which regular inspections were made by the police to ensure that it hadn't been driven within the town. Upon leaving, the car was escorted to the borough boundary by the constabulary, glad to see the back of Grose and his dangerous device.

1898 saw Grose's motor car business blossom. At the Motor Car and Cycle Show in February he showed Daimler, Leon Bollee, De Dion, and Benz machines. While he thought that the Benz was well constructed and he was selling several, it had some major weaknesses and he was convinced that he could improve it. Later that year, therefore, he ordered six Benz engines and countershafts from Mannheim and began to build his own chassis and bodies around them. The Grose chassis was tubular, of rather heavier gauge than the 'Ideal', and all the bearings were enlarged to accommodate ³⁄₈in. balls. A dogcart body was constructed upon it and handle steering was employed. These were marketed later the next year at £180 each, slightly more than the comparable Benz 'Ideal'. One chassis was given a van body and sold to Brice's of The Drapery, Northampton, a ladies' outfitters and haberdashers. Another was sold to Rootes of Hawkhurst.

An interesting sidelight on early motoring is that Grose also, like almost every other purveyor of motor cars at that time, offered driving instruction as a matter of course with any vehicle purchased. In practice this usually meant teaching a servant. The reduction in horses being kept by the wealthy meant that stable staff were being reduced. Redundant men were invited to turn chauffeur. As it was difficult for older men to turn their backs on a lifetime with horses, it was young stable lads who mostly turned to driving.

In 1898 Grose established another first in Northampton by becoming the first motorist in the borough to be fined for speeding. At 11.45a.m. on Monday 29 August he had been driving a car along the Wellingborough Road near the workhouse when he was spotted by P.C. Goodfellow who judged that the car was travelling 'at an extraordinarily fast rate', 15 or 16 miles an hour. It ran over a dog, he said, several times a collision was narrowly averted, and no bell, gong, or whistle was used. Both Grose, and his passenger Mr. John Hollingsworth, claimed that the car was only doing 8 or 9 miles per hour. Arthur Mulliner was called as an expert witness who stated that he had examined the car and it was capable of 16 m.p.h only on a decline and on a particularly good road. Such was the importance of this incident, the Chief Constable, Mr. F.H. Mardlin, presented the case himself. He stated that 'this was the first case of its kind that had been brought to the Court, and he had taken out the summons in the hope that there would be no necessity to prosecute anyone further'. Grose was fined £1 including costs.

The following year more firsts were notched up. The original 3½hp Benz-type Grose car, having been used for demonstration purposes, was sold to William Herbert Harrison, known familiarly as 'Jack', a tailor with premises next to St Peter's Church in Marefair, to replace a Darracq which he had earlier purchased from Grose. This Grose-Benz claimed the distinction of being the first motor car in Great Britain to be used by the police in the pursuit of a criminal.

The town was agog in April 1899 awaiting the arrival of the fabulous Barnum and Bailey's Circus, the Greatest Show on Earth. Four special trains were expected, bringing the show from Oxford, and a veritable tented town had been set up in fields near St James's Mill Road. On Thursday 27th, before the troupes arrived, a smartly dressed man visited several local shops distributing posters and offering, as was customary, complimentary tickets in return for their display. The system was, he said, to pay a

16 *The 1898 Grose Benz, later sold to Jack Harrison and used in the first police pursuit in Great Britain*

token sum for the 3s. tickets and have it refunded at the box office. Jane Botterill, at the little shop in Dallington, however, was suspicious and contacted Sergeant Hector McLeod at St James's End police station.

The man was last seen, he discovered, leaving town on the Weedon Road. McLeod promptly commandeered Jack Harrisons little car and they set off in pursuit. It is not recorded whether this was the officer's first ride on a motor car, but we can imagine the thrill of the chase, not to mention Harrison's excitement at being enjoined to 'scorch' in excess of the then speed limit of 14 miles per hour!

The suspect was overtaken and arrested near to Flore and brought back aboard the car. Frederick John Phillips, a con-man of no fixed abode, had forged the circus tickets and was charged with 12 cases of deception. For obtaining 10s. by fraud he was bound over to the sum of £10, a light sentence given under the First Offenders Act and taking account of his previous good behaviour. A small offence, perhaps, and a small penalty, but a significant step in motoring and criminal history.

That the Grose-Benz was an efficient little car for its day is evidenced by a letter in the *Autocar* of 6 May 1899. In a letter to the editor replying to a Mr. A. Valentine who had claimed his 33-mile non-stop run in a car as being 'the longest made by car on the road in England', Jack Harrison described a run which he achieved on the 19 April. It is a letter which gives a good idea of the state of development of the motor car at this time and of the very few drivers who were achieving long trouble-free runs.

Before eight o'clock he drove the car four miles out and four miles back. The morning being fine, and the roads in lovely condition, he determined on a day's drive. With a companion, probably Grose, he writes:

> Starting from Northampton at nine o'clock, we reached Coventry by eleven o'clock (Thirty-two miles non-stop). Round and about Coventry from eleven till four we reckon we did ten miles from Coventry to Warwick (ten miles) and we met you, sir, between Kenilworth and Coventry on your Daimler motor. We left Warwick a few minutes to six o'clock and arrived in Northampton before eight o'clock, non-stop being a run of thirty four and a half miles, making a day's run of ninety-four and a half miles. We intend trying a run from Northampton to Birmingham non-stop; if we do, we will let you know. In conclusion, I must say I am sorry for those who have been so unfortunate with Benz cars. I say, master them; what is weak make good. But above all, use good pneumatic tyres. Then you can do a non-stop run which is marvellous with a fascination indescribable. Motors have come to stay.
>
> Jack Harrison

That Grose and Harrison were motoring companions is plain, for they shared another 'adventure' in the latter days of May 1899; they were the first motorists in Northampton to commit a parking offence, being summoned for causing an obstruction in Bridge Street. The defendants left two cars in the street outside the *Pheasant Inn.* This caused a crowd to assemble, mostly boys, and although, in this case, they did not meddle, it might, the police claimed, have been very dangerous! The drivers had asked a patrolling constable if they could leave them for five minutes and were told that they could. That, the chief constable stated, the officer had no right to do, but the defendants had left them for a full quarter of an hour. He also said that he was sorry the constable had misled them, but he felt he was bound to bring the case forward. Constable Howes fairly stated that, although the cars were left unattended, after a time a young man came out and stood beside them. 'The cars were stationary, but the front one continually made a "chucking" noise', he said. After much deliberation the magistrates dismissed the case.

However, the matter raised a good deal of discussion in the motoring press. Police authorities claimed that the new Locomotives on Highways Act made no provision for motor cars to be left unattended. With horse-drawn vehicles a 15-minute allowance had been customary. An *Autocar* editorial contended that, as the Act provided that a car should not be left unattended unless the machinery was so arranged that it could not be unwittingly started, in all respects not dealt with by the Act the autocar was a carriage and reasonable permission in this direction was plainly contemplated.

As Whitsuntide loomed again Grose began contacting motoring friends and customers to assemble another demonstration of cars at Franklins Gardens. The reply from Mr. P.L. Smith of Walsall is typical:

> I presume that you are agreeable to allow me the same remuneration, viz. 10s., as before, dirt cheap at that, guv'nor! I am agreeable that it should go towards the money I owe you ... Would you mind seeing if there are enough tickets and what about 'Beware of Motor Car' bills?

So, the advertisements trumpeted, on the bill with Nana, Nano, and Nana the flying trapeze artistes, Mdlle Alma Beaumont the petit water queen doing fancy swimming and water walking, and Rivalli the fireproof man, was 'The Greatest Novelty of the Age, Horseless Carriages. MOTOR CARS will be at the call of Visitors, to carry them round the Cinder Track at a Nominal Charge'.

An interesting vehicle delivered to Grose about this time was a car built by Payne & Bates of Coventry, makers of Godiva gas engines, who, like Grose, had been experimenting with Benz-type vehicles since November 1898. Mulliner had bodied a Godiva wagonette, and perhaps Grose had seen the car there. Whether or not that was so, Grose ordered one of the firms new two-cylinder, four-seater, dogcart models.

Two

A New Century

In February 1900 the firm sold Grose Gear Case Company and established itself in premises in Pike Lane, off of Marefair, as Grose Limited. Here they adapted an old factory to make Grose Non-Skid Tyres, another of Joseph Grose's inventions.

As he often said in later years, it was the spinning of the little Motette on that initial excursion into town in 1897 that triggered off the invention of the Grose Non-Skid Tyre. Summoning up the old Northampton saying 'There is nothing like leather' and calling upon his skills as a currier, he devised a leather case into which was rivetted steel studs. This fitted round the tyre to give extra grip. He also produced for bicycles a lightweight version on 1¾in. tyres that consisted of a

17   *The Pike Lane tyre factory*

thin leather strip bearing two rows of shallow studs which was vulcanised on to a normal tyre. In tests conducted by the Cyclists' Touring Club they were found to be very effective in preventing what was commonly called 'the dreaded side-slip'.

Grose took out a patent on his non-skid tyres and bands. However, his other business interests were booming and needed his concentration. There were few cars about needing the treads and bicyclists tended to leave their machines at home when conditions were bad, so this side of the business was neglected and the patent lapsed. As the number of motor cars increased, though, the major tyre manufacturers universally copied Grose's idea and, 10 years later, he was rueing the loss of his patent, as one tyre firm alone was making a net profit of over £60,000 a year on such covers.

Not one to dwell on such matters, Joseph Grose set about improving his original idea. He had found, with the original cover, that as well as improving traction, the leather skin also reduced the number of punctures. Punctures were the plague of early motorists. The roads were scattered with nails lost from the shoes of horses and

21

18 *The Grose non-skid bicycle tyre*

thrown shoes and it was rare to complete a journey without having to repair at least one puncture. As few cars had detachable wheels this involved a roadside repair. Various ideas were tried to overcome the problem, detachable rims and the clumsy Stepney rim which clamped alongside the deflated tyre being two of them. Another difficulty with the straightforward leather non-skid cover was that friction between the cover and the tyre created heat which broke away the vulcanised layering of the tyre.

The problem of punctures was solved by packing steel studs so close that it was difficult for nails to penetrate between them, and the heating problem by building in an eyeletted rubbing strip beneath the tread which created a ventilated air space. This was patented No. 23481.

The Grose Non-Skid and Puncture-Proof Tyre worked extremely well, but it was an uphill struggle for Grose to

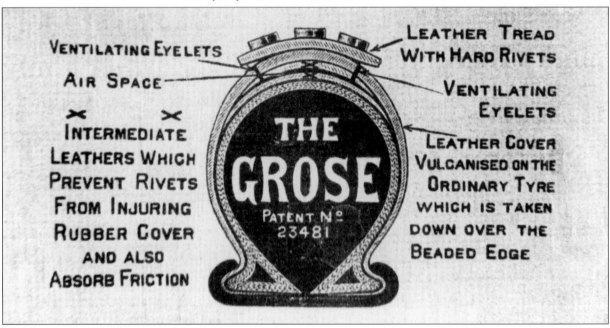

19 *A cross-section of the improved non-skid and puncture-proof tread*

20 *An amusing advertisement for the Grose Non-Skidding Tyre*

21   *King Edward VII boards his Daimler fitted with Grose non-skid bands at the Staff College, 26 June 1905*

popularise it as the big dealers offered great inducements to agents to push other patents in preference. In the early months of 1904 the Hozier Engineering Company of Bridgeton, an area of Glasgow, makers of the Argyll motor car, attempted a non-stop run from John o'Groats to Land's End with one of their cars. To minimise tyre troubles they fitted a complete set of Grose puncture-proof and non-skid tyres which performed admirably and were entirely trouble free.

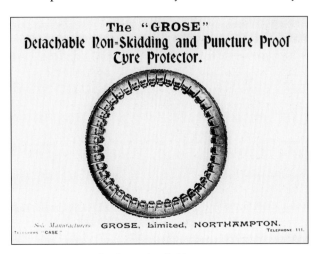

22   *The Grose detachable tyre protector*

In January 1905, in connection with the Automobile Show, non-slipping tests were held at Crystal Palace. On a surface liberally coated with a one-inch deep mixture of Thames mud and liquid soap, claimed to be the greasiest compound known, the non-slipping virtues of all the top makes of tyre covers were tested. On a granite incline beneath the first terrace five cars had to demonstrate turning, braking, starting, stopping, and restarting. Braking appeared to be the easiest and turning the most difficult of the tests. A Samson tyre fitted to a Germain car gained full marks in each trial, winning the competition. The Grose tyre was fitted to a

Vinot et Deguingand car scoring full marks for turning, 9 out of 10 for starting, and 7 out of 10 for braking. It was placed second, being awarded a bronze medal and £50. One has to feel sorry for the only motorcyclist competing in the event. Riding a machine fitted with Empire tyres he was unable to start on the incline as the surface was too greasy for him to get a foothold while in the turning test the rider was pitched one way and the bicycle the other. The rider, we are told, bore his fall with fortitude and scraped the grease from his garments with grim humour!

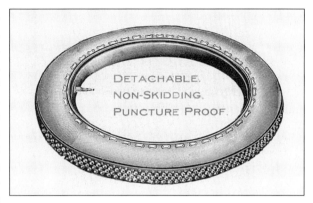

23   *The Grose No.1 detachable tyre jacket*

The resulting publicity brought the non-skid and puncture-proof tyres to the attention of important users, notably at the Royal Mews where Grose covers were fitted to the cars of their majesties King Edward VII and later King George and Queen Mary, H.R.H. the Prince of Wales, and Prince Christian. Orders poured in, too, from other distinguished motorists including Prince Hatzfeldt, Prime Minister Arthur J. Balfour, Lord Penrhyn, the Marquess of Camden, Lord Bolton, the Earl of Devon, the Earl of Northesk, Lord Lilford, Lord Elphinstone—the list is endless.

All motor taxi cabs licensed for hire in the London Metropolitan district, at this time, had to have at least one studded non-skid tyre fitted to a rear wheel and many of these were Grose's.

The construction of the tyres was interesting. In the Pike Lane premises were stored tons of best quality chrome leather specially bought in from the South of France because English chrome was too soft and less resilient than French hides and tannages. Initially, this leather was skived by hand but the introduction of machine-skiving speeded the process. Once cut to shape the wet leather was then stretched over a block and dried off to give it shape. Next the studs were inserted. Hardened steel rivets were packed so close together that the tyre was practically armoured and puncture-proof. Between four to eight hundred studs were put into each tyre, depending upon its size. This studded band was then cold vulcanised on to a standard tyre, either a new one or one of the customer's own. Over a ton of rubber solution, made on the premises by dissolving pure Para rubber in naptha, was being used a week at Grose's and the smell of naphtha was a characteristic of the Pike Lane area. After receiving 10 coats of solution the tread was then cold vulcanised to the tyre. This process meant that old tyres could be revitalised or repaired, Grose claiming that some had had up to twenty 'retreads' before expiring.

As well as the attached tread Grose also developed his Detachable Tyre Protector, designed for motorists who did not wish to use the fixed vulcanised studded tyres all the year round. This was a wider chrome leather cover that wrapped right round the tyre and either laced up by means of eyelets or had steel clips that were inserted between the tyre bead and the rim. These, too, were capable of having their treads renewed.

24 *The Grose 'Quick-Grip' motor cycle emergency gaiter*

Perhaps mindful of the poor motor-cyclist he had seen humiliated at the Crystal Palace trials, Grose also marketed motorcycle gaiters. These were, in effect, short lengths of the motor car non-skid cover. About nine inches long and slightly curved, this studded gaiter was wrapped around tyre and rim and the edges were laced together by means of eyelets. This, as well as preventing side-slip also, it was claimed, enabled a leaking tyre to be inflated enough to get you home. For non-skid use it was recommended that four were fitted to each wheel ... which must have made it feel like a square wheel!

During this time Joseph Grose was not neglecting his own motoring. He was getting about, covering large distances both for pleasure and business in a variety of cars. We find him on 29 August 1901, in London visiting his older brother Samuel, who had a butcher's shop in Campden Town. Passing through Islington, the canopy of his Panhard caught the over-hang of a fruit stall in the street market, knocking the whole structure over. He felt obliged to pay the stallholder 7s. 6d. compensation.

Always interested in what was being produced by other manufacturers and developers, in 1902 Grose somehow got involved in the construction of a Hyler-White steam car. This was an early do-it-yourself project run by the magazine *English Mechanic*. Designed by Thomas Hyler-White, son of a London silversmith who had worked for the Daimler Motor Company, plans were available from the publishers and instructions were printed in instalments in the journal. The necessary castings and other components were available from D.J. Smith & Co., engineers in the East End of London, and could be bought bit by bit as work or finances dictated.

One reader who resolved to have one of these cars was Captain H.L. Rokeby of Arthingworth Manor, near Market Harborough. Not feeling either inclined, or confident enough, to build it himself, he engaged the Northampton firm of J.T. Lowke & Sons to construct it. This firm, which eventually evolved into the world-renowned Bassett-Lowke model making concern, famous for their miniature steam railways, had their workshops in Woolmonger Street, just round the corner from Grose's premises.

With a wheel base of 7ft. 6in. and a width of 4 ft., the 'English Mechanic' must have totalled some 10ft. overall, a very large car for that time. Steam was generated

25 *Hyler-White's 'English Mechanic' steam car photographed at Lowke's workshops, Woolmonger Street*

26 *Grose is believed to have assisted with later developments of this steamer*

in a Serpollet-type flash boiler mounted behind the rear axle. The marine-style vertical twin cylinder engine was installed under the front seat, inches from the drivers posterior. It was discovered very early on that the engine vibrated excessively and strong steel braces had to be fitted to restrain it.

David Smith came to Northampton for the trial of the running chassis in June 1902 and commented that the workmanship was excellent: 'In fact the work was really too good in many parts'. After a run of two or three miles which took in Mulliners coachworks in Bridge Street and probably Grose's works also, Smith pronounced the car satisfactory.

Despite the close proximity to Lowke's of both Grose's and Mulliners, bodywork for the steam car was built by Messrs Salmons & Sons of Newport Pagnell at a cost of £40. Captain Rokeby ran the car briefly during that summer but in October he wrote that he was pleased with the result 'as an experimental car and a good strong knockabout toy … and we may be able to improve it into something better this winter'.

Photographs of the 'English Mechanic' trials were acquired and kept by Joseph Grose, and it is believed that he was responsible for some of the later developments of this car.

It may be that Grose's interest in the Hyler-White steam car was triggered by his exposure to another steam car that

27 *A Lifu steam carriage belonging to Sir David Salomans parked in Grose's yard. It was brought to Northampton for Grose to construct a wagonette body for it.*

28   *An air-cooled twin-cylinder New Orleans*

29   *A New Orleans complete with awning*

was brought to his garage late in 1901 or early in 1902 by Henry Greenly, a noted designer of model railways, a steam expert, and an associate of Wenman J. Bassett-Lowke who ran his model-making business in nearby Kingswell Street. Greenly had been invited by Sir David Salomans, ex-mayor of Tunbridge Wells, organiser of the world's first exhibition of horseless carriages in 1895, and ardent campaigner for motorists' rights, to help him get running an old steam vehicle that he had acquired. This was a Lifu, made in East Cowes on the Isle of Wight by the Liquid Fuel Engineering Company. After a disastrous maiden run in London when the vehicle ran amock, neither man quite knowing how to stop it, and steering complicated by a tiller system that turned the car left when the lever was pushed right, Greenly drove the steamer to Northampton where its wagonette body was given a covered-in cab in the Grose works.

It was during this activity that Grose made the acquaintance of former Lifu works manager H.G. Burford, now of Burford, Van Toll, and Company. This Twickenham firm made the Belgian Vivinus car under licence before making their own vehicles under the New Orleans Motor Co. banner. The result of this encounter was that Grose became agent for the New Orleans, selling a number of them locally, one being to Mr. Beard who had a similar bicycling background to Grose and whose business in St Giles's Terrace eventually developed into Abington Motors Ltd.

Grose Ltd. were very active at this time, constructing bodies on all sorts of makes of chassis. One of the firm's specialities was tradesmen's bodies of various types which were demountable and which could be replaced by a touring body for passenger carrying.

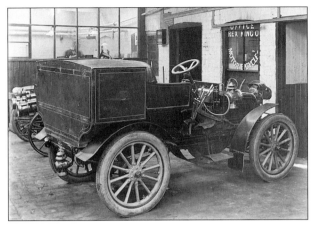

30 *A popular body style was the detachable tonneau and tradesman's box as seen here fitted to a 10hp Decauville chassis c.1906*

31 *Simple fixings allowed the commercial body to be removed and passenger coachwork attached when required*

32 *An early 8hp Decauville used as Grose's personal transport*

33   *W.T. Grose at the wheel of a Renault delivered in chassis form for bodying by Grose. Note that the two offside wheels carry Grose non-skid tyres.*

34   *1903 and a 14/20hp Renault carrying Grose two-seater coachwork is photographed in Mill Lane, Kingsthorpe*

As well as coachwork of their own design Grose's were also busy constructing motor car bodies for other well established bodyworks. Thus some coachwork bearing the plates of such makers as Starey's of Nottingham and Jackson's of London were actually made by Grose.

One of the better cars being produced at this time was the French Decauville, the make which inspired Henry Royce to build his first motor car. In 1903 Joseph Grose was using an 8 horse-power example as family transport. A photograph shows it with an ugly grilled radiator mounted somewhat incongruously ahead of the front dumb-irons. As early Decauvilles were distinguished by the horse-shoe shaped radiator mounted on the dashboard, could this have been a Grose modification? Whatever the case, Grose took on the distribution of the Decauville and sold many 8 and 10 horsepower models over the next five years, usually carrying his own coachwork.

It was about this time, too, that Grose started to forge links with the French firm of Renault, buying in a number of chassis upon which two-seater bodies were built.

On 1 January 1904, it became necessary for drivers to be licensed and all 'light locomotives', as cars were still designated, to be registered and to carry an 'identification number'. The letters allocated to Northampton Borough were DF and to

35 *Showing clearly the chain-driven wheels with drums for external contracting brakes*

the County BD. In the first 12 months 51 cars and 106 motorcycles were registered in the town and 179 cars, 13 heavy goods vehicles, and 305 motorcycles in the county. It was not long, however, before town drivers got fed up with small boys noting the DF and shouting 'Damned Fool!' after them. Representation were made and the letters changed to NH.

The weak link for most motorists was tyres and the search went on for better and more reliable makes. Towards the end of 1904 Grose took on the sole agency for Falconnet-Perodeaud tyres. This French make was already well known as heavy duty vehicle tyres but were now being imported as beaded edge pneumatics.

A regular source of work at the garage came in the winter months. Grose's had many customers who put their motor cars away for the worst months of winter. The vehicles would be left with Grose's who would strip them right down and prepare

36 *A 6hp De Dion illustrating the drawbacks of wooden wheels*

37 *Working on a De Dion engined motor cycle. On the left is a 6hp De Dion car and beyond a Panhard.*

them for the approaching season, even down to painstakingly stripping and revarnishing the coachwork. The service was the automobile equivalent of the old livery stables. Naturally, there was also a lucrative living in repairs and maintenance of both cars and motorcycles.

The firm was also operating a part-exchange scheme on new car purchases. To get rid of secondhand stock an auction sale was held at 1, Pike Lane on Monday, 24 July 1905. The cars listed are interesting and, in some cases, unusual. Heading the list was a 14hp Vinot et Deguingand giving 19 horse-power on the brake. A four-cylinder car with mechanically operated valves, four forward speeds and reverse, fitted with a side entrance body and a cape cart hood, the maker's list price was £600. It came complete with a pair of fine extra large Alpha headlights, three other lamps, and a quantity of spare parts. Was this the car that was used for the non-skid trials, perhaps? A second Vinot et Deguingand, a 10hp model with a tonneau body, was also offered.

An early 6hp car, possibly a Grose construction, merely listed as 'with De Dion engine' with a four-seater tonneau body, sold for 99 guineas. Grose had sold a number of New Orleans cars bought in from Van Toll of Twickenham and a twin cylinder seven hp example complete with canopy and side curtains, went for 40 guineas. Another twin, a 10hp Cottereau, seating five in a tonneau body, wearing new tyres fitted with non-skid bands, was sold to Victor Ashby of Towcester for 31 guineas. The French make of Turgan Foy was little known over here but a small six hp example, its all aluminium body seating three upon real leather seats, sold for 21 guineas. What must have been an early Panhard et Levassor, as it only wore pneumatics on the rear wheels, still carrying Counolby solid tyres on the front, went for 40 guineas. Of 6hp, it had a patent body seating four, a dais, and curtains. The sale was ended with a 3hp motorcycle also sold to Ashby and, representing the halfway stage between car and motorcycle, a 2¾hp Coventry Eagle Trimo powered by a genuine De Dion engine that came with all of the necessary parts, including spare wheel, to convert it back to a motorcycle.

That year, 1905, saw Grose again involved in the promotion of the S.M.M.T.s Motor Show but for the first time the show was held at Olympia and, uniquely, there were two such shows in the one year. The February event attracted 241 exhibits and

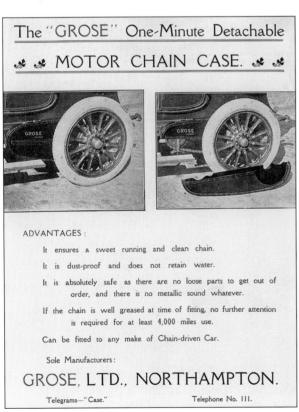

The "GROSE" One-Minute Detachable

❧ ❧ MOTOR CHAIN CASE. ❧ ❧

ADVANTAGES :

It ensures a sweet running and clean chain.

It is dust-proof and does not retain water.

It is absolutely safe as there are no loose parts to get out of order, and there is no metallic sound whatever.

If the chain is well greased at time of fitting, no further attention is required for at least 4,000 miles use.

Can be fitted to any make of Chain-driven Car.

Sole Manufacturers :

GROSE, LTD., NORTHAMPTON.

Telegrams—"Case."   Telephone No. 111.

38   *The Grose chaincase and lubricator for cars*

39   A Rover taxi cab, one of the first motor cabs on the streets of Northampton

the November one 269. The annual show was thereafter held in November each year until 1923 when it was moved to October.

Meanwhile, back at the works, development had been going ahead on the original Grose Gear Case and Lubricator. Although the original concept had been for bicycles it became obvious quite early on that the drawbacks to chain drive on bicycles also existed to an even greater extent on chain-driven motor cars. Grease on chains, when mixed with road grit and dust, became an efficient grinding paste and wore out chains and sprockets at an alarming, and expensive, rate. Larger versions of the covers were made for use on cars, designed to be detachable for inspection in one minute, dustproof and non-water-retentive, and rattle-free. A chain, well greased at the time of fitting, was expected to require no further attention for at least 4,000 miles, a claim confirmed by many testimonials from satisfied customers.

40   *Grose's hire fleet, 1909*

Among the many fine and luxurious motor carriages taken in part exchange and offered for sale in 1907 was one rather special racing car. It was an 8/10 horse-power Sizaire-Naudin light two-seater with direct drive on all three gears, a fast car. In the hands of French driver Georges Sizaire it had won the Coupé de l'Auto, a seven-day event in which the voiturettes had to attain high average speeds for six days to qualify for the race proper on the seventh. It had led for the entire race. In 1907 the same car had gone on to win the voiturette race at the Targa Florio meeting. After such a rugged career the car was advertised, justifiably, as shop-soiled! The price was £98.

It was in January 1908 that the *Northampton Daily Chronicle* announced: 'We saw a handsome £370 12hp landaulette which is to be placed upon the streets of Northampton tomorrow. It is finished in the most beautiful style, sprung, comfortably cushioned, seating four, and painted in dark green edged with white'. It was the first motor taxi to be introduced to the town. Grose had inaugurated the service in the face of a threat from out of town operators to flood the locality with London-style cabs. Grose explained: 'There is room for motor cabs as well as horse cabs. It's the country work, the evening work, we shall expect to cater for. You can take a journey with a motor cab which you can't expect a horse to take. We hope to ply from the taxi rank'. The vehicle was a Rover capable of 20 miles per hour and of turning in Gold Street. Fares were to be the same as the horse cabs. So successful was the venture that by July 1909 Grose's had eight cars and cabs for hire ranging from 12 to 40 horse-power, including Schneider, De Deitrich, Panhard, Rover, Renault, and Delaunay Belleville. With several other local firms competing for trade, they introduced a fleet of very comfortable Renault taxis at fares of only 8d. a mile.

As well as his business interests, Joseph Grose had, from the beginning, worked behind the scenes in the organisation of motoring. He was one of the 20 original bond-holders guaranteeing money for the first Motor Show at Crystal Palace in February 1903, having helped set up the Society of Motor Manufacturers and Traders the previous year, and was a founder member of the Northamptonshire Automobile

Club. Formed in 1906, the club had as members the cream of the county's nobility and gentry. Seventy members sat down to dinner at the *George Hotel* in October 1908 when the club, under its president Sir Thomas Fermor Hesketh of Easton Neston, played host to H.R.H. Prince Francis of Teck, the president of the R.A.C. Despite the Prince's patronage, the following year the club sent out a clarion call for support to combat irregular fines by magistrates, bad road surfacing, and inconsistent signing. Motorists felt that penalties imposed by magistrates were excessive. Fines were used for the relief of local rates, so magistrates were influenced to make fines greater than necessary. A report dated February 1910 stated that there were 535 motor cars registered in the borough and county, but only 88 members of the Club. To encourage membership the subscription was lowered from a guinea and a half to one guinea, and the entrance fee of 10s. 6d. abolished.

Many of Grose's contemporaries, pioneers of motoring, had moved on to become early aviators. When, on 27 April 1910, it became known that the French pilot Paulhan and the Englishman Claude Graham-White, had taken off flying north in the great *Daily Mail* London to Manchester £10,000 Air Race and were following the main London, North Western Railway line Grose set off post-haste in his motor car for Roade where Graham-White's Farman had been forced to land as darkness fell. Joseph Grose was an old friend of Bedford boy Graham-White having taught him to drive a car nine years previously. At Roade Grose was among the first to greet him. In an attempt to catch Paulhan, who had stopped overnight at Lichfield, Graham-White proposed to depart and continue in darkness. Grose organised other motorists to light the field with their headlights for take-off then guided the pilot by driving northwards. The English pilot left at 2.50a.m. Sadly, engine trouble forced him to abandon the race and Paulhan won the prize.

As well as their Rover connections, Grose dealt with Austins and become agents for Renault, a popular choice for wealthy businessmen hereabouts. James Manfield, the shoe manufacturer who lived at Weston Favell House (later to become Manfield Orthopaedic Hospital), had bought two, a 35/45hp and a 12/25hp. Mr. J. Sears, also a shoe manufacturer, likewise bought two, a 14/20hp and an 8hp. The 14/20hp was also the choice of Mr. Romer Williams of Newnham Hall. Sir Henry Randall, who lived at Monks Hall, just off the Wellingborough Road, preferred a British-built Standard, a six-cylinder 20hp car. Even the county set, fervently pro-horse, came round to the motor car. Both the Duke of Grafton and Earl Spencer, having strongly denounced the car and having announced that they would never have one, had succumbed to the lure of the internal combustion engine. The Red Earl, indeed, enjoyed motoring into his eighties.

In 1909 the government had introduced petrol tax at 3d. per gallon, but by 1910 there were 144,000 licensed vehicles on the roads of Britain. A year later and the official census indicated that there were 271 male and 1 female motor car chassis makers and mechanics in Northamptonshire, together with 234 male and 1 female motor car body builders.

It was grim irony that caused the 1911 Motor Show at Olympia to coincide with a strike of 6,000 London taxi drivers. Many old nags of horses, made obsolete by the motor cab, were dragged from retirement to pull ramshackle old 'growlers'. Joseph

41 *Joseph Grose's father, also Joseph, poses in an Austin outside the family home 'The Limes'*

42   *Pike Lane, 1912*

Grose, surveying the show from the gallery reminisced:

> It is marvellous, when you consider the youth of the motor industry. Fifteen years ago I went to a cycle show in Paris. There was one motor there, and it attracted very little attention. Who could have foreseen such a development as this? Now, Olympia is the Mecca of the motoring world, is even more successful than the Paris show, and there is a profit of £5,000 or more upon it.

As 1911 turned into the New Year of 1912 it was decided that the jumbled collection of old premises that formed Grose's works in Pike Lane should be demolished and a brand new garage erected. Several adjoining buildings were acquired and either adapted or demolished, including Dodd's mineral water factory, a small closing room, and some private residences. Some of the foundations dated from the time of the Great Fire of Northampton. While the workmen were excavating an old cellar in Marefair they came across a large cache of old port bottles covered with cobwebs and dust of indeterminate age. Although the corks had 'gone wrong', the wine, true to its virtue of improving with age, was found to be of precious quality, and was promptly transferred to the cellar of

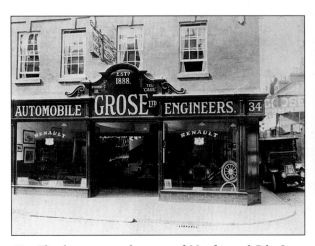

43   *The showroom on the corner of Marefair and Pike Lane, 1912*

44   *Renault and Rover are prominent in the showroom, 1912*

Mr. Grose. To whom did the port originally belong? Probably to the Reverend William Chancellor Wales, vicar of All Saints from 1833 to 1859, who had lived here in the days when a parson often prided himself on being a 'three bottle a day man'.

When opened in June, the new garage stretched the entire length of Pike Lane's west side, a distance of some 300 feet, covering an area of an acre and a half that had formerly been occupied by five factories. The portion fronting Marefair was a spacious showroom with 70 feet of plate glass set in an imposing mahogany fascia. A novelty was that the lettering on the windows was of real mother of pearl. This was a local invention and was the first example to be completed anywhere. In this area were displayed cars by Renault, Rover, Clement Talbot, and Maxwell. A special point was made of displaying Vickstow cars bearing Grose bodies. These were small chassis by Vickers and Bristow of London that were assembled here, mainly from American

45   *The 77ft. long corridor was a feature of the garage, 1912*

46   *A wide range of tyres were stocked including, in the foreground, Grose non-skids*

47 *A turntable was installed in the garage to utilise fully the space*

48 *A 1913 Rover 12hp with Grose 'Owner Driver' body*

49 *Convertible to an open car*

50 *Grose provided back-up on the Midland section of Ivan Hart Davies attack on the End-to-End record on 23-24 June 1913 in his 10hp Singer*

components, and sold for around £125. Only a very few two-seater Grose-bodied Vickstows were built, but the 1986cc monobloc engined cars were considered very attractive with their smart bullnose radiators. From the showroom a 77ft. long corridor inclined northwards along which were a suite of offices, a waiting room for ladies 'especially appreciated by those motoring in from the county who wish to remove the inevitable dust and deshabille of motoring in an open car', stock rooms etc. The corridor terminated in the garage proper, in the middle of which was a turntable to avoid the trouble of backing and reversing cars and to enable the best advantage to be made of the available space. The 14,000 square feet garage also contained a washing bay and three pits, one of which was 22ft. long by 6 ft. 6in. wide. The workshops, very well equipped with lathes, drills, shapers, a forge, presses for fitting solid tyres, etc., were capable of producing any type of spare part, even to cutting their own gears. Managing the garage was Joseph Grose's eldest son, William T. Grose, who had spent four years in the workshops at Rover and three years managing the repair department at Liverpool.

51   *1919 Calcott drophead coupé*

52   *The local contingent of the V.A.D. parade in Grose's garage during WWI*

Freshly opened, the garage added Darracq and Calcott agencies to their list. A special drive was launched to convince local tradesmen of the efficiency of delivery vans as, curiously, Northampton apparently had so few in operation. A Renault van similar to those used by Lyons or Swan and Edgar, or a Rover ½ tonner, it was said, with a Grose body, could be bought for £300. Running cost worked out at under 3d. a mile, less than half the cost of a horse.

While most of the larger cars were still delivered in chassis form and bodied to the wishes and whims of the purchasers or their chauffeurs, there was a growing tendency for owners to drive themselves. Grose offered their specially designed 'Owner-driver' body with Unit-Lock patented front screen. This was particularly popular built on the 12hp Rover chassis with worm drive back axle. Advertised somewhat optimistically as providing 'poppet valve efficiency with sleeve valve silence', the 22 brake horse-power monobloc engine would propel the car, it was claimed, from one to 50mph in top gear.

The firm's Rover connections led naturally to the adoption of the local Darracq agency when a range of models was announced designed by Owen Clegg, formerly

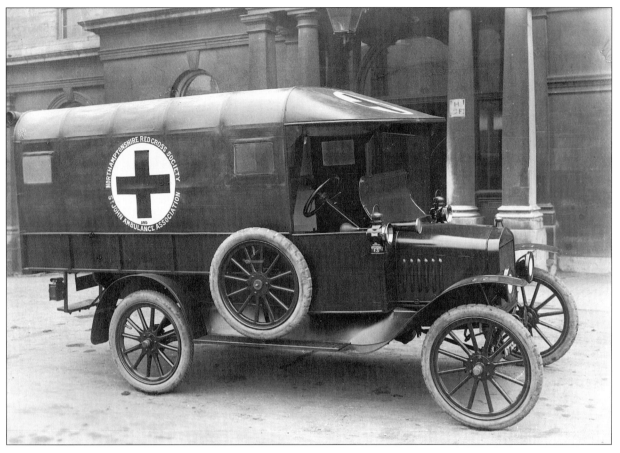

53 *Two-stretcher ambulance body by Grose on model T Ford. Seen outside Northampton General Hospital, 1914/ 1918.*

designer of Rover and Wolseley cars. Three models were marketed from Marefair, a 10hp two-seater at £185, a 12hp four-seater at £310, and a 16hp five-seater at £350.

For the impecunious there was a vogue at this time for cyclecars. Very simple and light and, it must be said, in some cases extremely primitive, they were an attempt to produce a car for everyman. In 1913 the well known long distance motorcyclist Ivan B. Hart Davies and passenger H.E. Govett made an attempt on the End to End cyclecar record. Grose fitted their Non-Skid Tyres to Davies's 10hp Singer which, on 23-24 June, covered the 886 miles in 34 hours 39 minutes.

Rather better than the average cyclecar was the Calcott, many of which were bodied by Grose at this time. Truly a light car with 65mm bore and 110mm stroke, giving it a nominal 10.5hp, it was available with standard works body complete with electric side and tail lights, but acetylene headlights, at £185. However, with Grose's smart two-seater dickey body, it became a very popular choice locally.

The company branched out on 16 July 1914 by forming the Northampton Motor Omnibus Company Limited with a share capital of £1,000, William Thomas and Percy Joseph Grose being named as directors, Kate Stanley joining them almost immediately as secretary and additional director. The company began by running a service between Northampton and Daventry with one vehicle. The bus ran 21,000 miles in the first eight months without losing one minute on the road and was highly successful. A second bus was purchased in April 1915 upon which a Grose 34-seater body was built. At the same time the N.M.O.C. bought a saloon motor-bus seating 24 to 30 passengers. This, too, was Grose-bodied, based on Pullman car principles, and fitted with electric lighting. With the comfort of passengers in mind, this vehicle had the then unusual sprung seats and backs, although it still ran on solid tyres and cast-iron wheels.

In their 1912 brochure Grose's had extolled the pleasures of motorcycling. 'Next to flying', they said, 'motorcycling is said to be the most exhilarating of all pastimes.' Grose had been selling two-wheelers since the early days, starting with the primitive Werners with a tiny Peugeot engine perched over the front wheel and driving it by a belt. By 1912 they were agents for Indian, Rover, and Calcott. To publicise this side of the business William Grose entered a B.S.A. in the Northants Motor Cycle Club's speed trials that were held at Moulton Grange Park in June 1914. As it happened, only one event was run, the meeting being cancelled when Mr. John Hooton, whose family ran Northampton's famous Penny Bazaar, riding a 3½hp James, crashed and was killed. Grose was fourth in this one event.

Somewhere about this time a Prince Henry Vauxhall, arguably one of the finest sports cars of all time, was purchased in chassis form by Mr. W.T. Badgery, chairman of the James Cycle and Motor Cycle Company. He designed for it a stylish touring body and commissioned Grose to construct it. The car's subsequent history is interesting. Registered in Ireland, it was in regular use until 1926 when Mr. Badgery replaced it with a sporting Chrysler and the Vauxhall was retired to gather dust in the garage. A young enthusiast by the name of Bert Greeves, who himself became famous in later years for his own brand of motor cycle, tried to buy it but could not raise the £50 asked. In 1945, recognising that the car was now a piece of history, Badgery gave the Prince Henry to Laurence Pomeroy junior, the technical editor of *The Motor*, whose father had originally designed this milestone of motoring for Vauxhall. This well known car was campaigned for many years by Pomeroy junior in V.S.C.C. events and probably inspired him to institute the Pomeroy Trophy competition which is such a highlight of the vintage sporting scene to this day.

The outbreak of war on 4 August 1914, and the imminent doubling of petrol tax to 6d. a gallon, seemed not to depress the car market. Everyone was convinced of British invincibility and, anyway, 'it would all be over by Christmas'. Grose decided to go ahead with planned extensions to the garage and in 1915 work commenced. The site of a derelict and dilapidated old shoe factory opposite the existing premises in Pike Lane had been acquired. The new garage of over 8,000 square feet had an entrance over 20ft. high 'so that a man wearing a high hat can stand on top of a double decker motor-bus and pass through without touching the top'.

As the war went on the workshops and garages of Pike Lane were more and more swamped in a sea of khaki. Armoured cars were serviced there, as were the many high quality staff cars requisitioned from civvie-street for the use of high-ranking officers. A considerable business was also done in converting private cars to ambulances. Many patriotic individuals and organisations donated cars. These came to Grose for ambulance bodies to be constructed before they were sent to the firing lines or to voluntary organisations. The firm also developed a two-wheeled ambulance trailer for use by the V.A.D. and similar organisations, a great number of which were built. Towed behind any car these carried two stretchers, were easily loaded, lightly sprung so that they were more comfortable than a motor ambulance, and were vibrationless. There was less noise from gears or engine, too, although one would imagine that exhaust fumes might be a problem.

Joseph's second son Frank James was an ambulance driver for the British Red Cross during the war and later served with the Royal Engineers. Joseph himself, his family, and staff who stayed at home all served with the Northampton V.A.D.

As the war reached a crescendo at Passchendaele and Cambrai in November 1917 news came that Joseph Grose's youngest son Lieutenant Albert George Grose, serving with the Royal Flying Corps, had been killed in active service during a flight over the Ypres salient.

Three

The Sunny Twenties

54 *Joseph Grose rides an A.B.C. Skootamota*

A wave of optimism swept through the motoring world as the war came to an end. Thousands of men were returning to civilian life having learnt to drive in the forces and, with a small gratuity, were looking for transport. At the north end of town Tom Wren purchased part of an old brickyard opposite the end of Balmoral Road to erect a big range of workshops for motor body building purposes. He intended, he said, to make new buildings 'in picturesque conformity' with the adjoining mock-Tudor Clarke and Sherwells printing works. This he did and the premises were soon occupied by the Northampton Motor Bodybuilding Company, the proprietors of which were Messrs Pittam and Crofts, formerly of 19 Thomas Street. When things got busy for Grose in the Marefair workshops, some of the coachwork orders were put out to the Kingsthorpe firm under strict supervision.

By 1922 the company had undergone a change of name to Croft's Motor Carriage Works Ltd. and Grose Ltd. had a more direct input both financially and from a coachwork design point of view. In practice many of the bodies leaving Croft's were Grose designs.

How motor vehicles should be taxed was a question exercising the minds of politicians at this time, too, and in 1919 the Ministry of Transport appointed a Departmental Committee on Motor Taxation which unanimously recommended a flat-rate petrol tax. The recommendation was rejected by government. Nearly 80 years on the idea is still mooted. As the following year wore on car manufacturers were becoming agitated by the Departmental Committee on Motor Taxation's new proposals that vehicles should be taxed on horse power, a suggestion vigorously opposed by the Automobile Association. Nevertheless, on 1 January 1921 a whole raft of new legislation came into force. Log books were allocated to each vehicle, petrol tax was abolished, but tax was levied according to 'horse power'. Not true horse-power, but a calculation worked out by the R.A.C. based mainly upon the bore of the engine, a formula which eventually encouraged many manufacturers to favour long-stroke engines. Payment had to to be confirmed by displaying a tax disc.

In the quest for economical transport for the man in the street several manufacturers, with expanded labour force and surplus machinery left over from wartime production, rushed out motor scooters. Most of these devices were very basic and some extremely primitive. Some were intended to be ridden standing up, a saddle being an optional extra! One of the better scooters was made by the Sopwith Aircraft Company and sold as the A.B.C. Skootamota. A mild sensation was caused, according to the local paper, on Wednesday 12 November 1919, when Frank Grose rode the first Skootamota into town. Apart from the toylike appearance, what surprised most onlookers was the ease of starting it. A quick push off with the foot, as with a child's scooter, and it was away, its little 1½hp four-stroke engine, mounted behind the saddle and over the back wheel, driving it smoothly. The chain drive was enclosed and ran in an oil-bath for long life and cleanliness. Weighing 65lbs. it was easily manhandled through passages and gates and returned 120 miles per gallon at 20mph.

As these little machines were popular, a race for them was included in the Northamptonshire Motor Cycle and Light Car Clubs speed trials that took place along the main drive of Castle Ashby Park early in 1920. The course was a flying kilometre with the timing line close to the start to prevent too much build up of speed before the timed section, in deference to the fact that a fatal accident had occurred during the last

55 *1919 two-cylinder, air-cooled Rover 8hp with Grose aluminium body*

56   *1919 Rover 8hp with Grose body and detachable top ...*   57   *... removable easily, the fore-runner of the modern sports hardtop*

speed event held here in 1908. Frank Grose won the scooter class on a Skootamota at 115 seconds, an average speed of 19.5mph.

The class for light cyclecars of 1,100cc or less saw P.J. Grose, usually known as Bob, finish second in an 8hp air-cooled G.N. behind C.H. Pettitt's 8hp Morgan three-wheeler. He went out again later in the meeting in the 750cc class, mounted now on a 4hp Indian motorcycle, for which the firm were distributors, and again finished second, this time behind Spencer Robb's 3½hp Norton.

This quest for economical and cheap transport caused the prestigious Rover concern to acquire the design of a light car from Jack Sangster, later to be chairman of the giant B.S.A. company. This little vehicle became extremely popular, selling over 16,500 in its five years' production. Powered by a 998cc air-cooled flat twin engine, the cylinder heads of which projected from each side of the bonnet, it came in standard two- and four-seater tourer, closed coupé, and light van versions. However, there was a demand for something a bit special in the way of coachwork, and Grose obliged by collecting bare chassis from the ex-munitions factory at Tyseley in Birmingham where they were made, and fitting them with lightweight aluminium two-seater bodies. Also popular was the version fitted with Grose's own detachable top, the forerunner of the modern sports hardtop.

Another lightweight that graced the Grose showrooms at this time was the Horstmann, handicapped in the immediate post-war period by its Teutonic sounding name; hence all Grose's advertisements appended the brackets '(All British)'. Described as 'the light car with perfect springing', and capable of 45mph and 50mpg of petrol, it sold for £155 with foot starter, adjustable pedals, and all accessories. The de luxe version with electric lighting cost 175 guineas.

In a booming market after the war but when manufacturers were not yet back in full production, Grose were happy to sell anything that they could get hold of, and took on many lesser-known makes. The list included the Detroit-made Chalmers, the Maxwell from the firm who took them over before both were swallowed up by Chrysler, another Detroit offering–the King, and the Briscoe.

58   *1921 Citroën shown at Olympia, with Grose two-seater coachwork*

In the commercial workshop they bodied a number of chassis by Chase after becoming sole Northamptonshire agents. Three models were available in 1-ton, 2-ton, and 3/4-ton versions, all fitted with David Brown worm wire drive back axles.

By the time the 1921 season came along Grose's were agents for the Malvern-built three-wheeled Morgan. The Northants Motor Cycle Clubs hill climb in June was run up Doddington Hill, from the tight bends close by picturesque Hardwater Mill, over the crossroads near the village, finishing on the brow. The course was 570 yards in length with an average of 1 in 7 gradient. Bob Grose won both of the light car classes, for cars under 1100cc and under 1750cc, with a smart little Morgan, Grose-bodied and with the then fashionable wheel discs.

The serious sporting events were interspersed with lighthearted fun, and the next weekend saw the Grose brothers at Franklins Gardens, where the Northampton M.C. & L.C.C. put on a gymkhana, doing well in events for skilful riding, the Victoria Cross Race, the Egg and Spoon Race, and Tilting the Bucket. The event was notable for one of the very first games of moto-ball ever to be played in Britain.

The 1921 Motor Show stand featured a neat little Citroën bodied here as a two-seater with dickey and finished in two-tone colours.

59   *1921 air-cooled, two-cylinder G.N. of 8.7hp with Grose aluminium sports body*

60   *A Grose bodied two-seater Alvis with dickey and Grose patent step ...*

Bob and Frank Grose continued in competition as the 1922 season began. The Morgan had given way to an A.B.C. light car and a Grose-bodied G.N. Bob had also acquired a potent 490cc Norton which he rode to success at the N.M.C.C.'s Why Not Hill speed trials.

A fortnight later Bob Grose was taking second place in the Club's 85-mile reliability trial driving the A.B.C. car. The tests included observed hills, secret checks and steep descents. Especially difficult, it was said, was the uphill hairpin turn on Napton Hill and the hill out of Priors Marston. The infamous Newnham Hill had to be climbed with limited speed.

For the 1922 show at Olympia it was decided to run with the current trend for the lighter cars and two of Grose's exhibits reflected this. On an 11/40hp Alvis chassis a sports two seater was constructed with an interesting dickey arrangement. Unlike most dickeys, where passengers had to step up the wings and over the quarters, this compartment extended forward ahead of the rear wings so that a fold-down door allowed easy access from the running board.

61   *... exhibited at the 1922 Olympia Show*

A concealed hood was also fitted. The unusual two-colour scheme of tobac brown over light drab, with antique leather upholstery and brightwork in nickel plate, was much admired.

Alongside the Alvis was a Grose all-weather body with a Beatonson collapsible head on the 12hp Rover chassis. Finished in amaranth red with antique red leather trim, it added extra colour to the stand. For customers who preferred a larger car there was a Dodge 17/24hp four-cylinder chassis carrying a Grose ¾ landaulette body. Special mention was made in the trade press of this car's very fine green and black finish.

Participating in competition was evidently good publicity. For the 1923 reliability trial Grose Ltd. entered two Alvis cars, a two-seater rather oddly carrying four passengers which lost only two marks and a four-seater fully loaded which lost but one. These were driven by W.T. Grose and works driver C.H. Harvey, both receiving silver medals. Bob Grose had forsaken his motorcycles for a smart Talbot Darracq which he took to first place and a bronze medal in the 1100cc class.

62   *The Wedford built by director Mr. W.E. Dickens*

63   *A smart limousine coupé body on a 1924 12/40 Alvis chassis*

Among the many luxurious bodies that were emerging from the coachworks at this time there was a curiously angular little sports two-seater. Based on a model T Ford chassis, it was built by Mr. W.E. Dickens the works director at this time. Related to Boddingtons, the brewers, he had worked for Alldays and Onions, the car makers, and joined Grose in 1908 from St Albans where he had a motorcycle business. Set off by disc wheels and a shallow radiator reminiscent of a Rolls Royce, the all aluminium body had not a single curved line in it. Registered as a 'Wedford' (W.E.D. Ford), its 23hp 95mm engine gave it a very sporting performance. The car subsequently languished in a corner of Grose's workshop until after the Second World War.

For the Motor Show Grose exhibited three widely varied styles. An Alvis Super Sports chassis with a 12/50hp overhead valve engine received streamlined sports two-seater coachwork similar to that shown the previous year, but with polished aluminium top deck and wings over dark red. The more conservative local buyer, however, perhaps preferred the sedate little limousine coupé that Grose constructed on the 12/50 chassis.

Less sporting, but popular with the family owner, was a four-door, five-seater all-weather saloon on a four-cylinder Rover chassis with a spring head covered with leather and cloth lined.

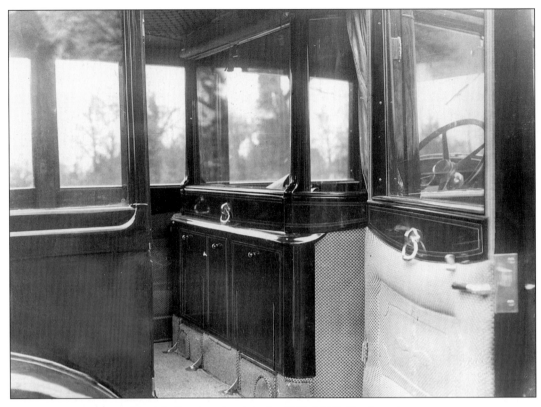

64   *The luxurious interior of a 1923 20/70 Crossley saloon*

More imposing was the 20/70hp Crossley sports-type chassis fitted with an en-closed drive four-seater saloon body. With a staggered V-front screen and fall in body sides, and frameless windows, its paintwork of kingfisher blue and steel granite, matched with velvet calf leather upholstery in harmonising colours, made it look deceptively small.

While the local press and the motoring journals were trumpeting Grose's more luxurious products, there was still plenty of work going through on more mundane chassis; on the bull-nosed Morris, for instance and the little Dodge.

Croft's Motor Carriage Works were having cash flow problems and, on 24 March 1924, went into liquidation with debts of £7889. Grose Ltd. bought the company and, for a while, continued operating it under the original name, the same designers, therefore, being responsible for both Croft and Grose bodies. Not only that, but Grose were sub-contracted to other coachbuilders, the

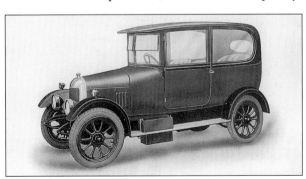

65   *Grose bodywork on the bullnosed Morris*

66 *Dignified coachwork for an 11.9hp Morris*

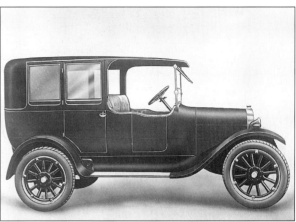

67 *Grose's 3/4 landaulette on a 1926 Dodge chassis*

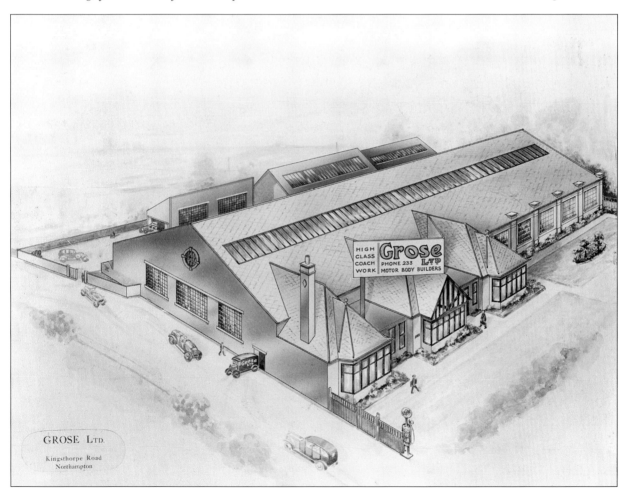

68 *Grose coachworks at Kingsthorpe Hollow*

69   *The Kingsthorpe bodyshop, October 1925*

70   *The paint shop at Kingsthorpe, 1925*

bodies going out bearing other makers' coach-plates. At the peak of production there were some 150 men employed in this part of the works alone. Among the makes which emerged with Grose coachwork were the Italian Fiat, German Steyr, French Renault, and English A.C. Mr. Croft went to Mulliner's where he conducted the final inspection of all bodies leaving the works.

The Marefair premises were gradually expanding, too, a number of ex-Royal Air Force wartime hangars being utilised for the purpose.

Something special was required, it was felt, for the 1924 Motor Show. On stand 85 Grose exhibited a stunning 15/40hp Darracq finished in powdered aluminium silver/blue

71   *Fiat 501 with two-seater and dickey body by Grose*

72   *Fiat 40hp chassis with Grose Pullman saloon landaulette body*

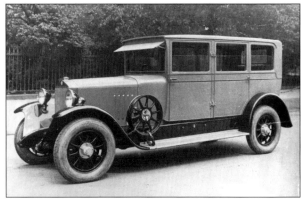

73   *Austere lines on a Steyr chassis*

74   *A saloon body on a Renault chassis leaves the Kingsthorpe works, 1924*

75   *Four-door sports saloon on an A.C. chassis*

76   *The Marefair garage, 1925*

over Parma violet. A two-seater with dickey, access to which was via Grose's patent folding side-step, it attracted much favourable comment in the trade press. Equally eyecatching was a sporting Talbot saloon alongside it finished in steel granite and kingfisher blue paintwork. A rich wine-coloured Lanchester 21hp four-door enclosed drive limousine added a touch of stateliness. This car featured an electrically controlled blind on the rear window and real down cushions concealed under the

77   *The turntable still features in this interior of Marefair garage*

top covers of the main seats. Completing the line-up was a 12/50hp Alvis Super Sports chassis fitted with a Grose streamlined two-seater body with dickey and Grose side-step. The outside-run plated exhaust added the final sporting flourish.

One of the racier things to emerge from Grose's works early in 1924 was a light-weight sports two-seater on a Vauxhall 30/98 chassis. Arguably, one of the best sports cars of the vintage years in standard trim, this version must have been a lively performer. With what was described as a Prince Albert body, featuring a 'beetle' back

78   *The tyre shop in Pike Lane, 1925. The ex-World War One armoured car, the Allchin steam lorry, and the lorry beyond are all on solids and are, presumably, awaiting new tyres.*

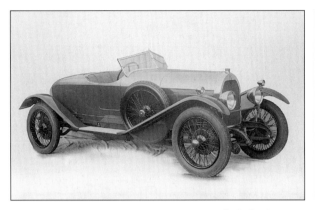

79 *Darracq 15/40 carrying sports two-seater body for the 1924 Motor Show*

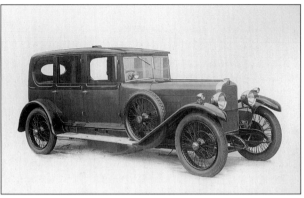

80 *A sporting saloon on Talbot's 1925 chassis exhibited at the 1924 Motor Show*

81 *A Lanchester 21hp chassis with Grose Pullman saloon body for the 1924 Motor Show*

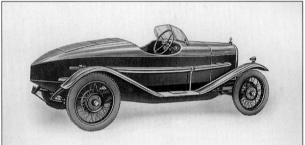

82 *Grose streamline two-seater and dickey on a 12/50hp Alvis chassis*

83 *Grose 'Prince Albert' body on a 1924 Vauxhall 30/98hp chassis*

84   *A box van body on a Ford chassis*

incorporating Grose's patent fold-down step with single-seat dickey, a straight-through, external exhaust pipe, outside handbrake, and finished with polished aluminium top panels over darker painted sections, its sporting aura was spoiled by an incongruous, old-fashioned Boa Constrictor bulb-horn. This car was illustrated in the *Autocar* magazine and Grose's brochure for the 1924 Motor Show. It would seem that the specimen car was delivered to a Stourbridge owner.

As well as stylish private car coachwork, Grose's were also busy in the commercial field, and one of the more unusual products in 1924 was for the Piano Galleries at

85   *A Grose box van body on a 1925 Maudslay chassis*

86   *A 1926 Chevrolet chassis bears a Grose box van body*

87 *£70 bought the box van body for this 1931 Chevrolet shown at Olympia*

88 *William Lloyd Grose, aged four, with his father and grandfather, as he tries his miniature Darracq racer*

32 Abington Street. The firm of G.S. Whiting & Co. ordered a low-topped box body, just large enough to hold an upright piano, on a model T Ford. Most of the commercial bodywork was, of course, purely functional but often featured beautifully sign-written panels.

Grose's list of agencies was extensive as 1925 dawned. As well as their long-established connections with Rover and Renault, they also held franchises for Buick, Crossley, Citroën, Chevrolet, Calcott, Darracq, Daimler, Dodge, Hillman, Lanchester, Talbot, and Trojan.

The early days of October 1925 saw a small car emerge from the Grose coachworks bearing the number plate WL 144. The vehicle was a handbuilt pedal car for four-year-old William Lloyd Grose, the son of Mr. & Mrs. W.T. Grose. The car was a scaled down replica of a Darracq racing car. The chassis was built at Grose's Marefair works and the body, with a polished aluminium top deck and smoke blue lower panels, was constructed at the Kingsthorpe Road coach works. Springing was by half elliptic leaf, steering true Ackerman, and braking on all four wheels operated by a hand-lever. Hartford shock absorbers, a Dover steering wheel, Wefco spring gaiters, outside exhaust pipe, and bulb horn completed the true-to-lifesize specification.

Stanley Sears, a wealthy local businessman and keen motorist, who lived at Eagle House, Cliftonville, Northampton had fallen in love with the Leyland Straight Eight after a demonstration run by designer Parry Thomas around the Brooklands track. As a result he purchased an open three-seater tourer, very basic, in undercoat grey. Although capable of over 100mph, Sear's car was seriously deficient in the stopping department, having brakes only on the back wheels. Sears had a new axle fitted to the front to carry brakes, which improved it slightly, although the tiny vacuum servo struggled to operate all four drums. This potent motor was a familiar sight around town, tractable though with a rich exhaust note. On the open road a second Zenith carburettor could be cut in to cope with the car's prodigious thirst. After a while Sears found the primitive body too stark even for a young man-about-town, so he designed an aerodynamic two-door sports saloon with a vee-windscreen, swept-down boat tail,

89   *A Grose sports saloon to the design of Stanley Sears on a 1925 Leyland straight eight chassis*

and aluminium side-step replacing the running boards and commissioned Grose to build it. An unusual touch was to bring in a craftsman grainer to reproduce the pattern of mahogany wood for the paintwork. The saloon, despite being a handsome head-turner, was, according to Sears, very disappointing and decidedly claustrophobic!

As Thomas intended it, the 40hp 7.3 litre Straight Eight was designed to be the finest luxury car available in the world and no expense was spared to achieve this aim. At well over £3,000 it was also the most expensive British car at the time. Not surprisingly, only 18 were ever built and two of them ended up in Northampton. At the same time that Stanley Sears bought the spartan racer from Parry Thomas his mother, who lived at Collingtree House, also bought a Leyland Straight Eight, the

90   *The design was adopted by Grose and included in their range of coachwork*

91   *A similar Leyland eight chassis was fitted with more stately Grose saloon for Mrs. Sears*

92   *Grose's Pullman saloon on a 1925 21hp Lanchester six-cylinder chassis*

smart Grose-bodied saloon that had been exhibited at Olympia.

The works pulled out all the stops again for the Motor Show. The *pièce de resistance* was an impressive 21hp six-cylinder Lanchester with Grose's six-seater Pullman saloon landaulette body, a staggered vee-type windscreen, and all windows in slides with a sliding division, all with special window-lifts doing away with handles as they were felt to disfigure the interior panelwork. To keep weight down, the body panels were in aluminium with no joints or mouldings, finished in dark maroon with black mudguards. Upholstery of the rear portion was in grey figured velour cloth, while the front section was in leather. Each internal panel was veneered from the waistline to the roof. All the cabinet work was in inlaid, polished mahogany, and included ladies' and smokers' companions. Blinds were fitted to all windows, the roof housed a ventilator, rope pulls and parcel nets were made of silk, there were electric roof lights front and rear, and electric telephone to the driver. A thick sheepskin mat adorned the floor and a modern touch was the installation of a Dictograph. A notable feature was the fitting of private locks to the rear doors so that the chauffeur could not avail himself of the rear compartment's luxury! It was a large car at 15ft. 6in. long and

93   *1925 Lanchester with Grose Pullman saloon body ready for the 1925 Motor Show*

5ft. 9in. wide, and cost £1,625 complete, or £550 as body only.

With it on stand 173 was a 17.9hp Renault chassis with a similar Grose Pullman saloon landaulette body but with the top portion staggered all round. Frameless glass windows were a feature. The interior woodwork was of antique mahogany fitted without the use of screws. Finish was in black top panels over olive brown. The price complete was £795 or, body only £400.

A 14hp Crossley completed the display, bearing an inexpensive five-seater saloon body. Although a four door design, the rear of the front seat folded forward to give unrestricted access to the rear compartment. Inside panels and fillets were of polished walnut, while the outside colour scheme was azure blue with black mouldings, mudguards, and chassis. The price tag was £615 complete.

It was a very different vehicle that joined the gleaming cars in the Marefair showrooms one Wednesday morning in March 1926. Battered and travel scarred and with a mantle of red mud, it was a 25/30hp Crossley truck, part of a group that had recently journeyed from the Cape to Cairo through the wilds of Africa in the hands of Mr. and Mrs. Court Treatt.

A new venture for the coachworks that year was the first of a fleet of motor coaches

94 *Renault's 17.9hp chassis was bodied in saloon landaulette style for the 1925 Motor Show*

95 *Unusually, the back of the front seats tipped forward on Grose's saloon landaulette body on a 14hp Crossley for the 1925 Motor Show*

constructed for Messrs du Cros. The first example was a 20-seater single-decker with a six-cylinder W. & G. du Cros engine and four-wheel brakes. At the time there was much criticism of Northampton town's few motor buses–cramped, solid tyred, and with slatted wooden seats. To make the comparison and with the hope of capturing some orders, the Grose coach was parked outside the Town Hall before being delivered to London. With a central aisle that allowed a six-foot man to walk upright, the floor and side panels carpeted up to window level, amply lit with electric lighting, and with fully sprung semi-bucket seats upholstered in brown antique leather, the local paper acidly commented that they made the municipal buses look like tumbrils! Smartly turned out in a new steel granite paint and wearing pneumatic tyres all round they glided along, so the reporter said, as smoothly and almost as silently as a swan on a stream!

96 *Grained overall to imitate sycamore wood, this sports saloon on a 20/98 Darracq Grande Sports chassis stunned visitors to the 1926 Motor Show*

On the subject of pneumatic tyres, the story is told of the first pneumatic-tyred bus operated by the N.M.O.C. making the journey to Stony Stratford. Driven under an arch into the pub-yard terminus with a full load of passengers, it was found to be impossible to leave when they alighted and the springs lifted. Stockley, the driver, had to deflate the tyres and recruit a crowd of passers-by to climb aboard and lower the bus to negotiate the arch!

The General Strike was affecting the town in 1926 when, on 7 May, Mrs. Mary Elizabeth Grose, the wife of Joseph George, died of pneumonia and rheumatic fever. Many of Grose's employees were out on strike but such was the regard in which Mrs. Grose was held that the church was packed with friends and workers.

As October approached thoughts again turned to the Olympia show. How to match the striking displays of recent years? The answer came in what the motoring press described as 'one of the most artistically designed sports saloons' at the show. Built on a 20/98hp Grande Sports Darracq chassis, this rakish car had a staggered vee-shaped front and rear, and staggered side pillars. The streamlining was carried through to a pointed tail and took in the petrol tank. The tail section was utilised as a tool locker, access being gained through a hinged squab. The interior was of polished mahogany with inlaid panels and burr walnut centres. The steps were of chased aluminium carrying hard white metal tread bars. But the most striking thing of all was the paintwork. A craftsman grainer had been brought in to reproduce in incredibly lifelike detail a facsimile of natural sycamore wood over the entire body and wings. So realistic was this that throughout the show people could be seen knocking the panels with their knuckles to determine whether they were actually wooden. This car was subsequently sold to a Mr. Berry and entered in the 1928 Southport Rally, winning awards.

Another Darracq, a six-cylinder 17/55hp with a ¾ drophead coupé body sat alongside its sister car. Not so stunning, perhaps, but attractive in black over blue with light blue leather trim.

For the luxury market Grose also showed an example of the latest 18/50hp Crossley long wheelbase chassis upon which they had built a 6/7-seater Pullman saloon landaulette body. Behind the driver's division the occupants, unusually, all sat facing forward. Upholstered in patterned antique maroon leather, its elegance was understated with light crimson-lake paintwork, black wings and top panels. The price was £975.

The diverse activities of the Grose operations were becoming something of an embarrassment by early 1927. The running of bus services in particular were time consuming, so it was decided to dispose of the assets of the Northampton Motor Omnibus Company. Overtures were made to the United Counties which were rejected. The Birmingham & Midland Motor Omnibus Company, operators of Midland Red services, were then approached. As a matter of courtesy, and as any acquisition of N.M.O.C.'s routes would bring the two firms into competition, Midland Red

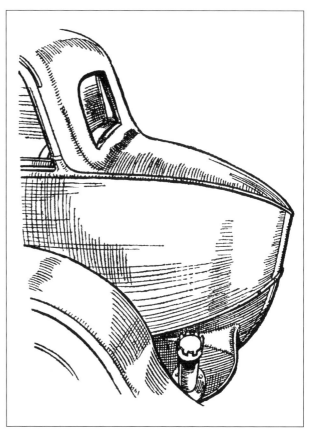

97   *The tail extension covered the tank and was utilised as a tool box*

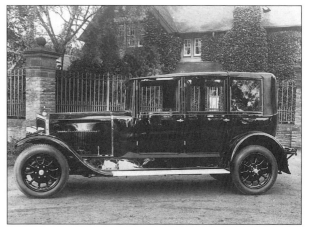

98   *A Dictograph, electric communication, and secretaire were fitted to this 18/50 Crossley landaulette Pullman saloon for the 1926 Motor Show*

99   *N.M.O.C. buses await passengers on Northampton's Mayorhold*

contacted United Counties. As a result Midland Red dropped out and United Counties picked up the offer.

The purchase included 45 licensed routes and 33 coaches, buses, and charabancs on a variety of chassis, mostly Daimlers and Chevrolet, but with odd examples of Clyde, Vulcan, and Graham. It is interesting that 19 of the vehicles were still running on solid tyres. United Counties continued to operate under the N.M.O.C. title until 1943, running routes daily to West Haddon, Welford, Lavendon, Stony Stratford, Lamport,

100   *Some of the N.M.O.C. vehicles, headed by a Graham Dodge coach, about to embark on a Grose staff outing to Wembley Exhibition*

Heyford, Weedon, and Daventry, as well as less regular services elsewhere.

The new bus bodies built by Grose the year before evidently impressed Northampton Corporation Tramways Committee, for four new single-decker buses were ordered on Guy B-type chassis. The mayor Councillor James Peach tried out the first one in early April 1927, declaring it the acme of elegance combined with durability and convenience. Even more extravagant was the newspaper report that 'the springing of the seats, which are in grey moquette, are calculated to make passengers linger after the terminus has been reached'. A novel feature was the arrangement that automatically reversed the seat in front of the emergency door so that, when operated, it formed a step down.

Buses formed a major part of the Grose display at the Commercial Motor Show at Olympia later in the year. A G.M.C. six cylinder 15cwt-chassis was shown with a 20-seater Grose all-weather body. The long hood was carried on special gearing to enable it to be raised or lowered at a moment's notice. All seats were of the semi-bucket type covered in antiqued leather and all windows were fitted with winders rather than with the then more common drop-straps. Finished in broken white and black it sold at £1,100 complete or £425 body only. A vehicle which attracted particular praise was Grose's 32-seater saloon bus body on a Tillings-Stevens B10A express-type chassis. All the strap-hanging rails and some fittings were covered in the locally made 'Doverite', a type of plastic coating, in brown. The interior was divided into two compartments, one suitable for reservation as a section for smokers. Tastefully finished in white and light grey with the mouldings picked out in dark grey, it sold for £1,488 complete.

101 *Grose's 'Fabricon' folding head was shown on a Darracq two-litre saloon at the 1927 Olympia Show*

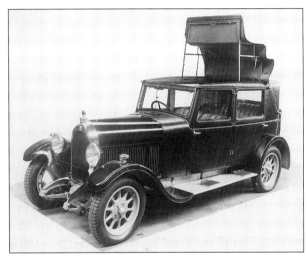

102 *The ease and speed of opening the cover was a great attraction*

103 *Also on the 1927 Show stand was a 3/4 coupé cabriolet on a Crossley 18/50 chassis*

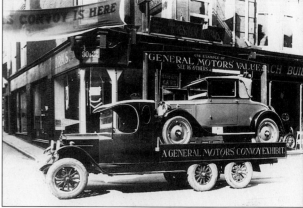

104 *Chevrolets head the General Motors Convoy visiting Grose*   **105** *A Chevrolet 25cwt. six-wheel truck carries a two-seater and*
in 1928   *dickey from the same maker*

Of course, the car shows interested the public most, and Grose ventured abroad to exhibit at the French Motor Show held at Le Touquet. The car that they sent to compete in the Automobile Club du Nord's *concours d'élégance* was the sycamore grained 20/98hp Darracq Six Special from the previous year's Motor Show, now slightly upgraded with such details as an Autovac roof ventilator, etc. The car took the premier prize for coachwork.

New coachwork on the two-litre six-cylinder Darracq chassis was kept under wraps for the Olympia show in October. Grose had devised a fabric covered body with their own 'Fabricon' opening roof. When closed it looked like a normal saloon with all studs and folding framework cunningly concealed. Opened easily, it became a full sunshine roof. The colour scheme was eyecatching with black fabric on the main body and black cellulose painted bonnet and wings contrasting with light grey paintwork for the chassis and the underside of the mudguards. Upholstery was in light grey leather.

A new marque for Grose's was Buick, and a particularly handsome example carried their enclosed drive limousine body on the Buick Master Six 25/75hp chassis. Finished in fawn over black, it embodied a number of American stylistic details such as light metal front pillars. In an attempt to silence that 'clunk' from the doors which so delights today's enthusiasts, the doors were hung on white metal hinges and fitted with adjustable dovetails and rubber silencers. Unusually, the roof and rear panel above the waistline were covered in black patent leather. Communication with the driver was by means of a Burovox telephone.

Groses were still selling Crossleys very successfully and the display included an 18/50hp six-cylinder chassis bearing a Grose ¾ coupé cabriolet. All the windows were lowerable on Rawling's cam-type grips and with spring lifts. A particular feature was the luxuriousness of the upholstery of the dickey seat. Stylishly finished in two shades of brown, finely lined out in yellow, the car was recommended, particularly, for shopping, as there was no dividing panel between the interior and the luggage carrier at the back so that parcels were easily accessible from the inside without removing the dickey seat.

106 *The Chevrolet 25cwt. farmers' general purpose truck and livestock wagon sold for £255*

107 *A Chevrolet box van pictured across the opening of Pike Lane*

108 *A Buick saloon and a show chassis occupy the Marefair showroom*

109 *An Oldsmobile chassis, in another window, still runs on wood spoked wheels*

110 *The General Motors display filled the Marefair and Pike Lane showrooms*

111   *… and looked even more impressive by night*

112   *In the garage were ranged Buick, Oakland, Chevrolet, La Salle, and Cadillac cars*

113   *A Grose saloon built on a 1930 model La Salle chassis for William Jackson of Leeds*

Advertising seems to have taken on a new importance in 1928. The year kicked off with a visit by the General Motors Convoy in February. This travelling motor show included the full range of Buick, Cadillac, La Salle, and Chevrolet vehicles. The La Salle, in particular, attracted a lot of attention, its V-8 Cadillac-based engine, low lines, and luxurious finish, all in what was a small size for an American car, captured several local buyers. Five examples were shown, ranging from a two-seater at £895 to a seven-seater limousine at £1,070. A nice saloon body was built by Grose's on a 28.8hp chassis La Salle a year or so later for a customer in Leeds.

General Motors followed up this successful promotion by sending another fleet of vehicles to the town in May, when observers were surprised to see a truck carrying two black and white Friesian cows heading the convoy. Realistically modelled in plaster, they illustrated the usefulness of the Chevrolet farmer's general purpose truck. Grose's coachworks had already bodied several G.M.C. chassis of various types and the convoy was joined on its excursions by 14-seater and 20-seater Chevrolet coaches, 20- and 26-seater G.M.C. coaches, and a special bodied chassis with an added axle to make it a six-wheeler, all bearing Grose bodies.

March, the month when, traditionally, motorists started thinking about new cars for the spring, saw Grose's long association with Rovers promoted by a week-long display of the full range that filled the Marefair showrooms and garage and was open until 10.30p.m. each night. Incidental to this, Rovers were demonstrating the fuel economy of their 10/25hp, the 'Nippy Ten', by undertaking a test, under Royal Automobile Club observation, to see how far could be travelled on £5-worth of B.P. spirit. By the time the car pulled up at Grose's it had been north as far as Glasgow and south to Devon, covering some of the most difficult roads in Britain. It had then completed 2,412 miles in the hands of two sisters, the Misses B. and N. Debenham.

Both the Rover and the General Motors connections were fully exploited at county agricultural shows in the region, where the light commercial ranges were displayed.

Guy had introduced in 1928 a new chassis suitable for bus construction in 1928. Designated the FCX, it was a forward control development of the C range and was

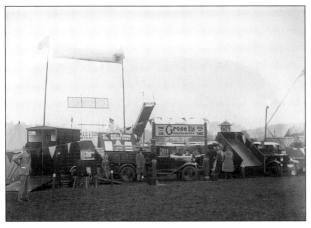

114 *The Grose stand at the Northamptonshire County Show*

115 *The Rover light van, the centre-piece of the Grose stand, sold for £260*

116   *Grose sporting coachwork on a 1928 20/98 Darracq Six Special*

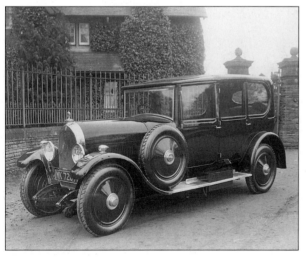

117   *Saloon body on a 1928 Darracq 20/98 Six Special chassis*

fitted with Guy's six-cylinder, side valve 7.6 litre petrol engine. Costing £1385 each, the N.C.T. purchased just one for evaluation this year. Registered as NH8496, Grose charged a further £725 for the body.

Out of the works, in 1928, rolled one car that even today still has enthusiasts licking their lips over the photographs of it. It was a 20/98hp Darracq Six Special carrying Grose's barrel-bodied four-seater open sport coachwork behind a large and impressive bonnet. Very reminiscent of a classic Bentley, it had much finer, more elegant lines than W.O.'s 'lorry'. More usually, the Six Special was bodied in more stately style as in the example produced that same year.

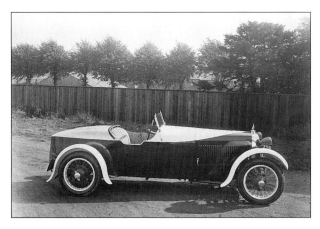

118 *Grose's 1928 show car on an Alvis front wheel drive supercharged chassis*

119 *Bill and John, with father W.T. Grose, in the supercharged f.w.d. Alvis at Brooklands*

120 *The first double-decker body by Grose for the Northampton Corporation, 1929*

121   *Grose fabric saloon on a 1930 model 20.9hp Vauxhall for the 1929 Motor Show*

As usual, the Grose coachworks came up with something startling for the Motor Show in October. Heading the three-car display on stand 107 was an 11.9hp super-charged front wheel drive Alvis with a Grose sports two seater body finished in dazzling black over white, the opposite way round to the usual two-tone style, and with white cycle wings and wheels. The body was valanceless and trimmed with real python skin upholstery. Will Grose himself took a liking to this car and, when the show was finished, used it as personal transport for a while. Indeed, in June the following year he took it to Brooklands for an Alvis rally where, competing in several races, he put up the fastest time of day, lapping the track at an average speed of 78.89 miles per hour with a maximum speed of over 90mph. His sons Bill aged eight and John aged five were passengers during the race and complained bitterly that Dad hadn't 'let it out' fully!

Alongside the Alvis on the 1928 Show stand was a 34 horse-power La Salle with Grose fabric saloon body, a design based on Weymann principles but contrived to avoid infringing patents. Finished in a curious putty shade, it also featured a set of trunks for the luggage grid covered in the same fabric material. The interior was lavishly panelled in inlaid burr walnut.

122 *Fabric covered, four-seat coupé on a 1930 model Marquette chassis*

123 *A 1930 light six Buick carrying a fabric sports coupé body*

124   *A fully fitted trunk and folding luggage grid made the Buick suitable for grand touring*

Completing the display was a 20hp Hillman Straight Eight saloon, beautifully finished in black and electric blue with upholstery in blue hide and figured silk material embellished with walnut panels.

While the show was going on news came through that a Grose-bodied car that had been in daily use for over two years had won first prize for its coachwork at the prestigious Southport Concours d'Elegance d'Automobiles.

The message had got home to Northampton Corporation Transport that excellent bus coachwork could be purchased in the town, and emerging from Grose's works in 1929 came the first of their double-decker constructions for the borough. Built on Guy three-axle chassis they had forward drive half cabs and faired-in rear wheels. The three-axle, six-wheeled, layout had been chosen after careful consideration as providing the best traction on the slippery setts that still paved some of the town's narrower streets. The two-axle, twin rear wheel, arrangement common elsewhere had been examined and rejected.

As the Roaring Twenties drew to a close, the last Motor Show of the decade was an all-General Motors display as far as Grose was concerned. Fashionable fabric-covering featured on all three bodies, a 20/60hp six-cylinder Vauxhall in sporting

125 *The aggressive frontal aspect of the Grose coupé Buick light six*

saloon style, the black being relieved by ivory coloured mouldings and leather, and a 23.4hp six-cylinder Marquette carrying sportsman's occasional coupé coachwork. The exterior was two-tone in stylish green and grey. Bucket seats were fitted at the front and an air-cushion bench seat at the rear.

Alongside them Grose showed a 28.8hp Buick light six chassis bearing a sports coupé body covered in sand coloured fabric, rather surprisingly matched with blue-painted wheels and mouldings.

Four

The Stylish Thirties

The new decade opened with a drastic change in the motorists law. From 1 January 1930, it became compulsory for all drivers to hold third-party insurance cover. At the same time recognised signs, signals, and practices, which had become more or less standard over the years, were enshrined in the first published *Highway Code.*

By 1930 customers were increasingly opting for the standard bodywork options from the factories and foregoing the luxury of bespoke coachwork. True to their reputation for selling only the better offerings from the industry, Grose's fought the 'baby-car boom' by becoming distributors for the Triumph Super Seven. Coming in 11 different versions ranging from the open tourer at £162 10s., through fabric saloon, sallandaulette, and Tickford saloon, to the supercharged sports at £250, they were one of the best of the small cars but sadly overpriced for the market they were aimed at.

Despite this, there were still some delectable motor cars going through the workshop to be enhanced with fine coachwork. A vee-radiatored Mercedes was fitted with a fabric two-door, four-seater, sports coupé body. Carrying very little weight, this car must have been a real flyer.

In the mid-market range Grose's were featuring the lowest priced British Straight Eight engined car, the Hillman. The Straight Eight and its sister model the Fourteen were each available in seven versions including a Six-Light Weymann fabric bodied saloon. The full Hillman range was on display at the garage in February 1930. Featured strongly in the advertising was the Segrave Model at £495, named after the then holder of the World Land Speed Record, Major Sir Henry Segrave. He visited Grose's premises with Captain J.S. Irving, technical director of Hillman's and designer of the 'Golden Arrow' car.

Following closely in the Hillman's tyre-tracks, the next exhibition at the Marefair premises was the 'Top Gear Exhibition' a title recently resurrected by the popular TV motoring programe for its annual show at Birmingham. The 1930 display,

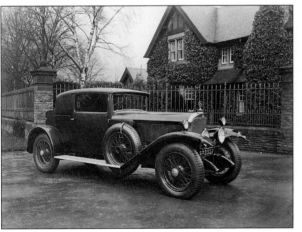

126 *A 1930 Mercedes chassis carries Grose fabric sports coupé bodywork*

however, revolved around the Buick and Marquette range sold under the slogan 'the top gear car'. Buick, a big car by British standards, offered a model named the 'Empire' saloon at £485 for this country. The Marquette range, also made by Buick, was the smaller, cheaper offering with prices from £310.

As was their custom, Grose's offered their own coachwork on the Buick, and an example constructed for a Miss A. Thornely of Eastbourne was entered by that lady in the prestigious Eastbourne Concours d'Elegance. This annual event attracted some of the south of England's smartest cars and the Grose-bodied Buick took first prize for cars costing between £500 and £800.

127 *A prize-winner at the 1930 Eastbourne Concours d'Elegance was this Grose-bodied Buick*

A significant development for 1930 was the introduction of a whole new range of Grose-designed bodies on popular chassis. These were a sort of halfway stage between

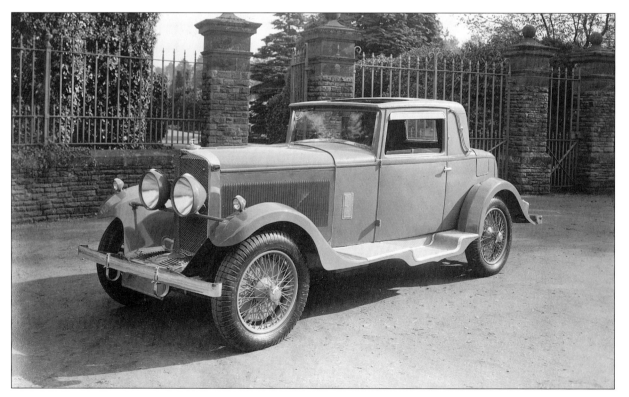

128 *Talbot Ninety for the 1930 Motor Show with sports coupé body*

129   *The dropped step was a feature of this car*

130   *Again Grose favoured the pointed tail on their sporting bodies*

131   *Grose's patent folding step allowed easy access to the dickey seat*

the fully custom-built coachwork of the past and the standard factory options then coming off the production lines. Each body, exclusive to Grose though built to a common design, was available on a choice of chassis and exhibited the flowing lines that were characteristic of Grose coachwork. As the wood that formed the framework of the first offerings in this range came from local woodlands, it was decided to name them all after Northamptonshire villages. The idea may have been inspired by another local firm, Watts of Abington Street, baby carriage specialists, who had earlier marketed their own range of perambulators with similar local village names.

The first to be marketed early in 1930 was the 'Braunston', probably so named in honour of Mrs. Joseph Grose's birthplace. Initially this was intended for the two-litre 15.7hp six-cylinder Rover. While the standard sportsman's saloon, as produced at the factory, had just been reduced in price to £368, Grose's 'Braunston' saloon version cost £50 more. First to buy one was local councillor Mr. James Peach; the car was registered NH9875.

The Motor Show rolled around again in October and on stand 92 Grose's were displaying three examples of Grose coachwork on Rover, Talbot, and Buick. The most significant of these was the Talbot Ninety. This car was chassis number 29911, bought from the works on 29 July 1930, and was a short wheelbase AO90. Upon it Grose built a fixed head, fabric bodied sports coupé with a dickey seat in the sweeping, pointed tail. Access to this was by means of a Grose patented fold-down step. This, when closed, formed a section of the side and top panels. Finished in pale green and cream, it was a rakish car featuring a dropped step section in the running boards, dummy hood irons and a flush fitting sliding roof. All the exterior fittings were chromium plated, a modern trend replacing the old nickel plate, a move not popular with all motorists at the time, it has to be said. Upholstery was in matching pale green and the interior was trimmed out in walnut. The car bore the price tag of £675.

After the show the car was registered as PL3312 and sold to an unknown customer. He must have been a keen motorist, for he fitted it with an extra reserve 7½-gallon fuel tank as well as many other accessories. Having covered 34,000 miles in just about two years the car ended up in the hands of Warwick Wrights, the Talbot distributors, from whom it was purchased by the late Peter Hampton, the noted 'Bugattiste'.

The new owner immediately added many other extras to the already comprehensive list of accessories. As the car then weighed in at some 33cwt., handling was affected and some modifications had to be made to improve road holding, but nevertheless it was capable of 0 to 50mph in 13 seconds and of lapping Brooklands consistently at close on 80mph. Hampton kept the car for 18 months during which he added another 31,000 miles to its total, a good many in competition.

Grose's did good business with Talbots. Between mid-1930 and late 1936 they purchased 56 Talbots from the works, 10 of which were in chassis form to be bodied in Northampton.

The body exhibited on the eight-cylinder 26/45 horse-power Buick chassis was a close-coupled four-seater fabric covered coupé finished in black and grey cellulose. Priced at £445, it was shown with fitted safety glass, an optional extra at £8.

Fabric again featured on the Grose body fitted to the show Rover. This car was a two seater drophead coupé built on the 19.3hp six-cylinder Light Twenty chassis and its cellulose paintwork was in two shades of brown.

Grose coachwork also featured on other stands at the show. Rolls Royce displayed an imposing enclosed drive, four-door, six-light saloon on the big 40/50hp chassis. Designed to be light and airy, it boasted large windows of Protectoglass, although the louvre ventilators over the four doors attracted some criticism from purists who felt that they spoiled the lines of the sleek grey and black body.

Joseph Grose, the founder of the firm, had by now more or less relinquished control in favour of his sons and, in January 1931, celebrated his 70th birthday with a party at St James's church institute for all parishioners aged 70 or over. Over two hundred turned up to be entertained by some notable local figures, including the then mayor, Councillor Harvey Reeves, who was a leading figure in local light opera circles. The birthday cake was appropriately adorned with a pennyfarthing bicycle and a modern motor car.

The commercial side of the coachworks was thriving, especially the construction of coach and bus bodies. Grose's contacts with Citroën put them in an advantageous position when from 1928 the French firm widened its commercial interests. When, in the autumn of that year, Citroën announced their new range of commercial vehicles to complement the existing light vans, Grose constructed a number of interesting variations upon lorry chassis and even Kegresse half-track chassis. In February 1931 Citroën introduced two new long wheelbase chassis, developed from the familiar 35-cwt. model. With the wheelbase extended by some three feet, one version was intended for goods use and had single tyres on all wheels, spring

132 *An updated design for the Corporation's new buses on Guy six-wheeler chassis*

133 *An advertising body for the Dominion Dairy Company on a Morris Minor chassis*

dampers at only the front, and the fuel tank under the driver's seat. The passenger-carrying chassis had dual rear wheels, 30 x 5-inch tyres all round and hydraulic damping fore and aft. A 16-gallon fuel tank was mounted under the rear of the frame. The 2442cc six-cylinder 19.3hp engine had a four-bearing crankshaft with vibration damper and aluminium pistons, all in unit with the gearbox. Grose designed a new 20-seater coach to suit this chassis which met with Citroën's approval. From then on Citroën's illustrated the Grose coach in their catalogue and offered it from their Brook Green sales office at £495, the lowest price of any 20-seater then on the market.

By the time the Commercial Motor Show came round in November the Citroën commercial chassis had been uprated by enlarging the engine bore from 72mm to 75mm. Now carrying new low pressure balloon tyres and Grose's new 20-seater body for it, it was the centrepiece of Citroën's stand.

Citroën's commercial venture in the UK was shortlived, however. When the popular front wheel drive cars were introduced in 1934 the factory concentrated on this model, surrendering the UK commercial field to Bedford, Chevrolet, and others.

Northampton Corporation Transport had evidently been well pleased with the double-decker buses built by Grose in 1929 so that, when they purchased new Guy chassis in 1931, they ordered identical 54-seater bodies again, the only difference being that, when slightly larger tyres were fitted, the rear wheel fairings were dispensed with.

As Northampton entered the new decade it awoke to the need to attract industry to the town. To promote this it was decided to commission a film showing the town's commercial activities and its attractions. Directed and edited by Mr. Bassett-Lowke and shot by members of the Northampton Cine Club, the film included shots of work in progress in Grose's body shop. It was, of course, a silent film. When, in the 1980s, the film was rediscovered and a sound commentary was added, this segment was mistakenly attributed to Mulliner's, but has, in the most up-to-date version, been rescripted correctly. Interestingly, the film shows one of Grose's more unusual vehicle bodies under construction. To the order of the Dominion Dairy Company of Aylesbury, a fleet of advertising bodies in the shape of country cottages was fabricated on Morris Minor chassis to publicise 'Chilvern Cottage' cheese.

On the buyer's instructions, these were to be built as quickly and cheaply as possible. The work was put into the hands of George Lacey, a Mulliner-trained craftsman coachbuilder who, like many similarly skilled men, shuttled back and forth between local firms taking short-term employment wherever the work was. He was told to select a small team of apprentices and less skilled men. They were paid a small bonus for speed, Lacey 1d. per vehicle and the men ½d.

About the same time a body looking like a giant pack of Germstroyd 'the super spray germicide essence' was constructed upon a Hillman Minx chassis.

Brief stages in the production of a coachbuilt car body are shown in this film and it is, perhaps, appropriate here to describe the construction in more detail, as it was done at Grose's.

134 *1932 Hillman Minx chassis carrying a Grose advertising body*

Vehicles arrived in chassis form, driven from the factory by works drivers muffled to the eyes in scarfs and leather coats with flying helmets and goggles as protection from the cold. An old wooden box served as a makeshift seat and a sack strung up on two sticks, over which the driver peered, gave a modicum of protection from driving rain.

The coachbuilding work-force was organised into gangs of four or five men, each team responsible for the complete construction of a particular body.

Weathered timber was purchased as required, much of it from the local firm of Travis and Arnold in St James's End, and, during the period when the 'village' series of bodies was being marketed, was supposedly from local woodlands. Mostly ash, this was stored in the yard at the rear of the building. Once brought in, it was first planed to remove the inevitable warping and reduced to the required thickness. Then, depending upon which body was to be made, the shapes were marked out by means of brown paper patterns, the skill of the craftsman being to get as many pieces as possible from the plank, given that the grain had to run in the right direction to withstand any stress. An intimate knowledge of wood growth and properties was necessary here.

After the wood was cut to shape on a band saw, the appropriate bevels and joints were cut. Joints were usually very simple mortise and tenons or half-joints. The mortises were cut on a spindling machine, as shown in the film, and screw holes drilled.

Assembly was usually done direct on the chassis by joiners who adjusted joints by hand to get perfect fit before fixing them permanently with screws and angle-plates, glue being used very rarely. This was an extremely important stage, as any sloppiness here resulted in the body rapidly developing creaks and cracks once in use. After assembly the woodwork was giving a brushcoat of preservative.

Panels, whether of steel or aluminium, as in later cars, were first roughly shaped by hand with wooden mallets on sandbags then smoothed on rolling machines before finally being hand planished. In the very first days of Grose bodybuilding much more hand work was done, but mechanisation came in very fast.

Attachment of the panels was by brass pins for silence. The final stage was minute inspection of the skin for dents and blemishes; any found were corrected by hand. In the paint shop the first necessity was to wash down the whole body with warm soda water to remove fingerprints and grease. In the early days it was common to apply 17 coats of primers, coach-paint and varnish all by hand, but by the heyday of Grose coachwork cellulose had mostly taken over, applied by spray and cured in drying rooms. All rubbing down was done by hand.

Leather for upholstery, as you would expect in Northampton where the world's best skins are appreciated, was in top quality Connolly hide. Joseph Grose's early experience as a currier was a prime factor in acquiring the very best. Skins were marked out from templates similar to those used by the local 'clickers', cut in the traditional way, and stitched into seats and panels. Seats, which usually were constructed with springs and horsehair stuffing, later gave way to wadding or the patent pneumatic cushions that became something of a craze in the late '20s and '30s. Interior panels were often stitched and pleated in typically art deco designs–sunray patterns or geometric motifs. Final trimming consisted of the addition of polished wood cappings, dashboard and similar items, the majority of which were French polished by hand on the premises.

It is interesting that one of Grose's intro-
ductions in 1931 harked back, in termin-
ology at least, to the very early days. They
introduced a 'travellers brougham' into the
light commercial range. Unlike the earlier
version which was simply a sample carrying box grafted on to a car body, this was
in reality a straightforward light van and a
Bedford chassis, albeit fitted with a low
clerestory roof.

A Talbot Ninety again featured on the
Grose stand at the 1931 Motor Show. This
time it was on the AM90 long wheelbase
chassis number 32815. To illustrate the
speed at which Grose's painstaking craftsmen turned out a showpiece, this Talbot
was delivered as a chassis on 20 August
1931. It was complete and ready for the
Show in the early days of October. This
six-cylinder Speed model foursome coupé
carried a Grose close-coupled, two-door,
body with a luggage boot at the rear. Safety
glass was fitted throughout in anticipation
of the new law, due to come into effect the
following January, requiring all new cars
to be so equipped. Finished in restrained
colours of fawn and blue cellulose, it was
upholstered in fawn furniture hide piped
out in blue. The price complete was £787.

The large 15/18hp Lanchester that
joined it on Grose's stand number 102 was
less staid than the usual coachbuilt saloons
constructed on this six-cylinder chassis: a
sign of the times. Described as a sports-

135   *Drophead coupé bodywork on a 1932 model Rover Pilot
chassis for the 1931 Motor Show*

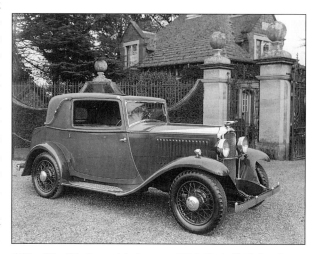

136   *The 'Harlestone' body on a 1932 Vaxhall Cadet chassis*

type coachbuilt saloon seating 4/5 and with a four-door body, it was finished in the
fashionable contrast of ivory and black with deep brown furniture hide for the upholstery. Interior woodwork was polished walnut. The price was surprisingly cheap at
£732 complete.

The third offering on the show stand was a 12.8hp six-cylinder Rover Pilot coupé
known as the 10/25hp. This was another in Grose's notable 'village' series. The
'Kingsley' was a two-seater drop-head coupé with a dickey seat at the rear, the show
car fabric covered in green with sports hooding to the head, buff mouldings and
wheels.

The 'Harlestone' also appeared in 1932, Grose's sports four-seater coupé with
dummy pram-irons designed for the Vauxhall Cadet chassis. The 16.9hp Cadet had

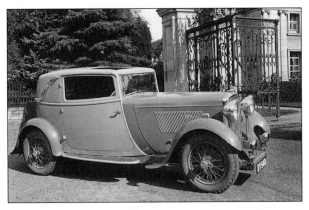

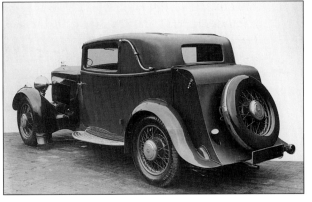

137 *Sports coupé bodywork on the Rover Meteor light twenty chassis*

138 *The tail of the Grose sports coupé on the Rover Meteor chassis*

been announced the year before and marketed as a cheap six-cylinder, the first Vauxhall with synchromesh gears.

Sporting lines were very much in mind when, in February 1932, a new body was designed by Will Grose for the Rover Meteor Light Twenty chassis. Features of the body were that the waist moulding was swept to conform to the lower edge of the body panels, alongside which were swept elongated steps. Swept lines were also

WHEN MOTORING WAS IN ITS INFANCY

The Name of

Grose Ltd
NORTHAMPTON

STOOD FOR GOOD CARS & SERVICE.

Higher than ever it stands for the

SAME TO-DAY.

Vauxhall	Rover
Talbot	Triumph
Alvis	

"Ancient and Modern."   The GROSE Exhibit in Northampton Carnival.

GROSE LTD. MAREFAIR, NORTHAMPTON.
Telephone 2111.   'Grams "Case."

139 *Ready for the 1932 Northampton Carnival, the Rover Meteor with Grose's 1909 Renault*

reproduced in the back of the large luggage trunk and in the flow of the rear wings. The tail of the car was clean, with the dumb irons, chassis and tank all covered in and the spare wheel encased in a metal cover. The bonnet was made longer than standard, giving a racy appearance, although a small scuttle was retained. Streamlined sidelamps were mounted atop the rigid, close-fitting front wings. The exterior colour scheme was subdued in two shades of mole, while the upholstery was in moquette over inflatable air cushions.

The first week in March Will Grose with W.E. Dickens, Grose's service manager, as navigator set off for Norwich in the Meteor, from which starting point he was heading for Torquay in the British 1,000 Mile Motor Rally. The pair set out at 6.14p.m. on Tuesday 8th to finish at 10.21a.m. exactly on the Thursday. Now more cheerfully finished in brown and green with the engine painted in a matching green and rather curiously equipped with a barometer, illuminated ashtrays, and a folding table, the Rover also had a 'clutch specially arranged to slip' which enabled it to put up 'a wonderfully good show both in the slow running and acceleration tests'. They finished a creditable 9th in class 1 against a formidable entry of works cars.

In June Mrs. W.T. Grose took the car to Heston Airport, in those days second only to Croydon as a flight terminal, for a prestigious rally organised by Messrs Henly's. Primarily a *concours d'élégance* the event was strongly supported by the *Motor* magazine. Grose's car was awarded two prizes, the first in its class and a silver cup for 'the most outstanding car' presented by the *Motor*.

Perhaps the 'slipping clutch' arrangement was handy, a few weeks later, when the car took part in Northampton's annual Cycle Parade. With Joseph Grose, the firm's founder's bicycling background, both he and the company had supported the local Cycle Parade since its inception in 1890. Held each summer to raise funds for Northampton General Hospital, by 1932 it had grown to include motor floats and other vehicles. Grose's had recently acquired an Edwardian car, a 1909 Renault. This car, registered NH463, had originally been supplied new to a doctor at Weedon. Like so many young men, he had volunteered for service during the First World War and, like other serving motorists, had garaged his car at Grose's for the duration. Sadly, he did not return. The Renault, and several other cars with a similar tragic history, languished in a corner of the Marefair premises until the early '30s when the re-establishment of the London to Brighton veteran car run awoke the public interest in historic motor cars. As an advertising ploy the 1909 Renault was entered in the Cycle Parade, together with the 1932 Rover, as 'Ancient and Modern'. Today the car still survives in J. Grose's showrooms, lovingly cared for and fondly described as 'as new, having one previous owner'.

In a spirit of rivalry, Mulliner's entered their veteran Daimler in the Wellingborough parade that same week. This car truly was a historic car, being the very car that had been owned by Colonel Mulliner and demonstrated by him at Buckingham Palace in November 1897 to the Prince of Wales. Once again, however, the date was mis-stated, this time an earlier date was quoted–1896. Then, to compound the error, the *Northampton Independent*, in it's report of the event, stated that it was the first car in Northampton. This brought forth an immediate response from Joseph Grose in a contradictory letter to the editor which was published in the next edition. This car, happily,

140 *Grose's single-deck design on a 1932 Dennis chassis for Northampton Corporation*

still survives in the loving care of a Veteran Car Club member.

Meanwhile, though, work went on at the garage and the coachworks. Northampton Corporation Transport extended its suburban services with the addition of single decker 24-seaters designed and built by Grose on Dennis chassis. The showroom was making great play with the Triumph Super Seven, remedying some of its old shortcomings by improving access with a four-door pillarless saloon at £157 10s.

The coachworks had continued their village series with a new body on the Rover Gazelle chassis. Called the 'Coton' it was, once more, a sportsman's fixed head coupé and very similar to the body that had been so successful on the Meteor. Mrs. Grose,

141 *The 'Coton' body on a Rover Gazelle chassis won honours in the Eastbourne Concours d'Elegance in the hands of Mrs. Grose and Miss Hessie Phin*

accompanied by Miss Hessie Phinn, companion to Mr. and Mrs. Stanley Sears, took the car to the Eastbourne Concours d'Elegance. The ladies wore fashionable dresses and hats in harmony with the two-tone finish of the car, which carried some interesting accessories. Above the windscreen, central to the roof, was a front-facing direction indicator, a housing that exhibited left and right arrow-shaped lights to oncoming traffic. These units were only just being introduced, mostly on American cars, and then only on the rear. On the Grose car this fitting was surmounted by a Viking's head mascot as befitting a Rover. Mounted on the offside windscreen pillar and operable from the driver's seat was an adjustable spotlight. Chromium plated horns and red-lensed warning lights added to the impressive front view of the 'Coton', while the fabric covered luggage boot was fully fitted out with purpose-built cases. The car won prizes in every class in which it was entered.

Talbots figured strongly in the output of the coachworks at this time and the 1932 Motor Show saw Grose's again giving prominence to a Talbot carrying their own coachwork. This time it was a 'Ninety-Five' in continental coupé style. A two-door close-coupled four-seater, it was finished in straightforward black cellulose with wheels and moulding in brown, a more subdued colour scheme than was usual for Grose show cars.

Two sports saloons stood alongside, both Grose bodied. One, on a six-cylinder Vauxhall Cadet, was finished in two shades of mole and green, upholstered in crushed grain green leather, and carried the price tag of £335. The other was a sweeping four-door body on a 12hp four-cylinder Alvis Firefly chassis. The 1496cc Firefly was a replacement for the 12/50 and was to become generally available for

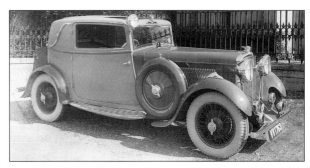

142 *The offside of the 'Coton' showing the sidemounted spare in colour-matched cover*

143 *For the 1932 Motor Show Grose built a close-coupled continental coupé on a Talbot Ninety Five chassis*

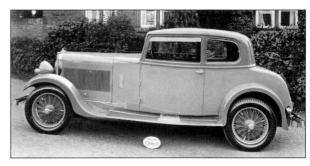

144 *A 1933 model Talbot Ninety chassis with Grose sports saloon body*

145 *The 'Sywell' four-door sports saloon on an Alvis Firefly chassis*

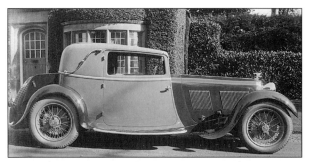

146   *A two-door sports coupé body, shown at 1932 Olympia on a Vauxhall Cadet chassis, but here fitted to an Alvis chassis*

the 1933 season. The Grose body continued the village range by being called the 'Sywell'. Although finished in muted colour scheme of two shades of grey, the car was highlighted with blue wheels and mouldings and blue leather for the interior. Simple and elegant, it won the I.B.C.A.M. Silver Medal in section 3 of the Private Coachwork Competition. The price complete was £570.

Announced at the 1932 Motor Show was another Alvis chassis, the Speed Twenty, to be in production the coming season. This created considerable interest and Grose immediately announced that they would be supplying the 'Sywell' coachwork, slightly modified, on this new model also. Grose's sweeping style suited this Alvis with its new low-slung chassis and six-cylinder engine developed from the 20 horse-power Silver Eagle.

At the same show, but on the Rolls Royce stand, was exhibited another example of Grose coachwork. This was a beautiful enclosed limousine with a rakishly low roof line mounted on a 45/50hp Phantom II chassis. This was identical with a design drawn up and built earlier that year especially for Mr. E.V. Bowater, the son of the ex-Lord Mayor of London.

Grose's show stand at the 1933 Olympia show seemed to lack some of its usual style. Again three cars were exhibited. The usual Talbot was in evidence, again on the

147   *The interior of the Alvis sports coupé*

148   *Grose enclosed limousine on a Rolls Royce Phantom II chassis*

Ninety Five chassis but the coachwork did not carry the Northampton firm's charac-teristic sweeping lines or stylish flair. The full-panelled continental-type saloon was decidedly chunky in side elevation and heavily over-tyred. The all-black paintwork, even though relieved by chrome mouldings, did not help. The price was shown as £779 10s. including the Ace spare wheel cover.

It was a relief, then, to find that Grose's 'Brampton' body on a 14hp Vauxhall Light Six chassis had nicer lines. The four-seater sports coupé de luxe, as it was decribed, confusingly carried a Pytchley sliding roof. This roof was a bought-in speciality from another Northampton coach firm, the Pytchley Autocar Company of Bradshaw Street. Grose's had, in the planning stage tentatively called one of their village series of bodies the 'Pytchley', but to avoid confusion the name had been dropped before production started. The show car was finished in duo-tone cellulose of mid-blue over grey lower body panels. The darker colour was car-ried through for the fabric-covered luggage trunk, fully fitted out, at the rear. The rear window blind, so long a feature of all cars

149   *The 'Brampton' four-seater coupé on a Vauxhall Light Six chassis*

and usually operated by a pullcord running through eyes, had been abandoned in favour of what was called Purdah glass in this body. Customers wishing to accentuate the trademark Vauxhall bonnet flutes could have them chromium plated for an extra 30 shillings.

The third car on stand 13 at the show was a Vauxhall Big Six 20hp chassis carrying Grose's transformable coupé body. This had a collapsible head that converted it to either an open coupé or a coupé de ville. The deep fawn main panels were contrasted with green lining-out, wheels and upholstery.

150   *A detachable and fully-fitted trunk was part of the design*

The stand at the 1933 Commercial Motor Show at Olympia featured another coach for the local firm of Yorks, operating under their title of the 'Easy' Coach

151   *The Grose stand at the 1933 Commercial Motor Show*

Company. A Maudslay ML3H forward control chassis, it bore a Grose 32-seater, rear-entrance body finished in two shades of blue and carrying chrome mouldings and flashes.

Popular motoring novelties of the day were the little Rytecraft miniature cars that were being built by the British Motor Boat Manufacturing Company at their London works. Vauxhall commissioned a number of these little vehicles and fitted them with tiny versions of Vauxhall bodywork, complete with the trademark fluted bonnet. Grose's brought one of them to Northampton in November 1934 as part of a travelling Vauxhall display team. Powered by a 1hp engine and capable of 12mph similar

152   *The little Rytecraft car with a miniature Vauxhall body attracts a crowd on Northampton's Market Square*

cars could be bought for £70. To launch the exhibition the miniature car was driven

153   *An open tourer built on a model AW75 Talbot chassis*

154   *A Grose-built articulated pole truck at Hardingstone Junction power station*

by local child film star June Holden. She had recently completed the film 'Lorna Doone' playing the child Lorna to Victoria Hopper's adult role. The film featured Margaret Lockwood in her first film part and was due for release that Christmas Eve after a Royal Command showing.

There was still plenty of demand for craftsman-built bodies on private cars, although pure one-off custom-built coachwork was becoming rare. The scene was different, though, in the commercial field. Each trade required a particular type of vehicle and Grose's commercial section was kept busy supplying their needs. 1934 saw some interesting vehicles leave the works. An articulated pole-truck for transporting the 30ft. long or more wooden poles then used for carrying electric power cables was constructed for the Northampton Electric Light and Power Company, based at the Hardingstone Junction generating station. The Commer tractor unit was so constructed to double at other times as a short-bodied flatbed truck.

With safety glass becoming available in increasingly large sheets, a travelling showroom was built on a Commer chassis for Campbell's furnishing stores. The vehicle was fitted out with over 150 lights, which necessitated rigging a special generator. It was used to tour the many new housing estates springing up in the '30s, showing off three-piece suites and other household furniture.

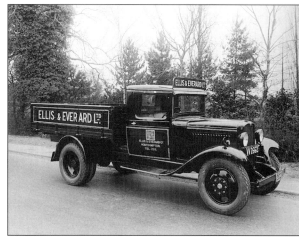

155   *A travelling showroom on a 1934 Commer chassis*   **156**   *Elaborate lining out on a dropside bodied Bedford*

Ellis and Everard Ltd., the builders' merchants, ordered a normal dropside body on a Bedford chassis. Nothing unusual in that, but the signwriting must have given the poor painter a headache for the whole vehicle was lined out with thousands of little letter 'E's!

Coaches figured prominently on the stand at Olympia for the Commercial Motor Show. The Grose 20-seater built on a Commer N3 chassis, despite its glittering paintwork and chrome flashes down the side panels, still exhibited the traditional layout of flat screen, projecting bonnet, and wings. It was overshadowed by the sign of things to come, a 32-seater streamlined de luxe coach on a Maudslay SF40 chassis, built for F.A. Sugden's Bestways Coaches. The show vehicle had a sun saloon head capable of being folded right back, seats in full moquette, and was finished in striking red, blue, and black paintwork. Its windcheating 'teardrop' shape and absence of projecting parts made it a popular choice of operators and several were built with minor variations for such fleets as Hall Brothers and the Northampton-based Easy Motor Coach Company, now known as York's.

The village series continued with versions intended mainly for Vauxhall chassis. Their Light Sixes, in 12 and 14hp options, had developed from the Cadet and had been in the showrooms since 1933, to be joined in 1934 by the Big Six, the 3.2 litre that became such a mainstay of Vauxhalls range that it was in production until 1937 when it gave way to the popular 25hp with independent suspension. First shown at the 1934 Motor Show was the 'Coton' body now revised for the Big Six. A four-door sports saloon, it came with a

157   *A Commer N3 chassis with 20-seater body exhibited at the 1934 Commercial Motor Show*

158   *A de luxe coach built on a 1935 Maudslay chassis in what Grose employees came to call the 'teardrop' shape*

fabric covered dome roof and quarters and a concealed sliding roof. A steel luggage trunk graced the back, fully fitted out with a top tray to accommodate a canteen container, while the lower section was fitted with two specially constructed suitcases. With the lid of the trunk in the down position it was strong enough to serve as a luggage grid. The spare wheel was mounted in the nearside front wing encased in a thief-proof metal case. Both front doors carried Vauxhall's 'No-draught' ventilating

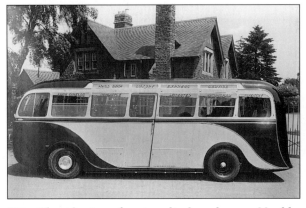

159   *The side view of a streamlined coach on a Maudslay chassis for Hall Brothers*

160   *One of two streamliners delivered to York Bros. 'Easy' Coaches in April 1935*

161   *The 'Coton' body was adapted for the Vauxhall Big Six chassis for the 1934 Motor Show*

windows. A sign of the times was that the windscreen wiper motors were now secreted below the scuttle and that the trafficators were flush in the door pillars.

Very similar in style was the 'Weldon' which followed almost immediately. Intended for the Light Six and also a sports saloon, it differed from the 'Coton' by carrying its spare wheel externally mounted on the rear luggage trunk, rather than on the front wing, again covered with a steel case.

The third in this village trio was the 'Alderton', a two-door fixed head coupé based on the Big Six. Although basically similar to its sisters, with fabric domed roof and quarters, a rather more sweeping tail and sloping rear side windows gave it a sportier look. All three cars were trimmed in best Connolly hide, the door panels stitched into a fashionable sunray design, each model distinctive and different. The slightly lower roof line was compensated for by building recessed seat wells affording comfortable legroom for passengers. Both of Grose's Light Six models sold at £399, in the case of the 'Alderton' for the two-light version. A four-light option was available which put the price up another £11.

To join these three bodies there came a quite different construction, and likewise on the Big Six. This was a transformable coupé based upon the Motor Show car of the previous year and now called the 'Lamport'. The head, in light canvas contrasting with the paintwork option, could be folded back to coupé de ville position or right down to the waist rail, making it an open tourer. The interior door panels were stitched, in the case of the 'Lamport' in art deco style with a bold geometric design of

162   *The 'Weldon' body designed for the 1934 Vauxhall Light Six chassis*

163   *The 'Alderton' fixed head coupé for the Vauxhall Big Six, seen here in its four-light version*

164 *It was also available in de luxe form with chromed headlamps, extra trim, and direction indicator lights instead of trafficators*

diamond pattern and the mouldings, which on the other three models were merely described as 'polished wood', were burr walnut on the 'Lamport'. Naturally, this extra quality was reflected in the price which was £425.

The principles incorporated in the 'Lamport' appealed to the family motorist with sporting inclinations and there was a demand for a similar body on a better chassis. Rileys had a reputation for excellent performance on the road and, with modest tuning, in competition. This, matched to Grose's 'transformable coupé' body, would produce a first class, long-legged tourer. The result was the 'Burcote', built on the Riley Kestrel chassis and shown at the 1936 Motor Show.

A Grose body emerged from the works about this time the design of which fore-shadowed present-day trends. Built on a 1935 Commer chassis, it was an estate car remarkably similar in concept to today's 'people movers'.

It was always with sporting carriagework that Grose exhibited most flair, and in 1936 a particularly elegant drophead coupé body left the works on a 4½ litre 30 horse-power, six-cylinder Invicta chassis. Although the lines were very understated, they suited the rather square profile of this handsome 'low chassis' car.

Although Grose did not body many Lanchester chassis, Mulliner's were the local agents for the make, they, like most other garages, would acquire and clothe any make

165   *The sunray pleated leather panels were standard, but alternative patterns were available at the customer's choice*

166   *Also on the Vauxhall Big Six chassis, the 'Lamport' transformable coupé*

167   *Shown at the 1936 Motor Show, the 'Burcote' drophead coupé body on a Riley Kestrel chassis*

of chassis if the demand was there. Thus they constructed a very attractive sports saloon on a 1936 Lanchester 12hp Light Six chassis.

A very different product was a dignified hearse body built upon a 25hp Vauxhall chassis in 1937. Although it was not a type of coachwork undertaken very often by Grose, they had in the past built hearses on Armstrong Siddeley, Daimler, and, more surprisingly, the little Citroën.

As the '30s progressed, and in the aftermath of the depression, those wealthy enough to have afforded custom-built coachwork in the past preferred to keep a lower public profile, so ordered the excellent standard bodies available in great variety from the large number of manufacturers. The fine craftsman-built motor carriages were now constructed either for formal use or for the habitués of Nice, Cannes and similar watering holes, where elegant ostentation was almost a requirement.

The first of Grose's models to suffer was the 'village' range designed for the Vauxhall Big Six. The arrival at the showrooms of the '25' in February 1937 emphasised just how good a production-line car could be. For £298 the customer got a powerful 25 horse-power six-cylinder car capable of 80 miles per hour and excellent acceleration for such a hefty vehicle. Independent front suspension gave a smooth ride while so-called 'double safety' hydraulic brakes took care of stopping. Ventilation, at long last, was built in and did not rely upon opening vents and quarter-lights. Semi-bucket front seats, labelled by Vauxhall as 'Body-Conformity' seats, controlled synchromesh gears, an adjustable steering column, and 'Pedomatic' starting, were all part of the

168   *'Float-on-Air' seats with individual armrests featured in the 'Burcote's interior*

standard specification. A big, roomy car with a 48in. wide rear seat, it provided plenty of leg, head, and arm room for five people.

Similarly, Rovers, with whom Grose had had close associations since their bicycle building days, announced their new Sixteen sports saloon. It fairly bristled with refinements and sold at a competitive £370. Riley, set firmly in their traditions, nevertheless introduced their 1½ litre, while Talbot, that mainstay of Grose coachwork, showed their newest production-line version of the established 'Ten' in the Marefair showroom. This latter model, in tourer form with Grose-built coachwork, was chosen by Mr. and Mrs. W.T. Grose for their entry in the Empire Exhibition Scottish Rally in 1938. Finished in a striking gun-metal grey with grey leather upholstery, it won first prize, a silver salver and silk banner, in the class for open car coachwork after completing the gruelling rally course in the Highlands.

As ever, in the commercial workshop things were still buzzing. An unusual construction was a special elevating platform unit devised for the Northampton Gaslight Company upon a Bedford chassis in 1937. This enabled workmen more easily to service the new tall street lamps that were proliferating along the town's main highways. Being motorised, it also speeded up the operation, a facility that was put to good use a couple of years later when the wartime blackout descended on the town and street lamps had to be dowsed almost overnight.

The local St John Ambulance Brigade were badly in need of a new ambulance at this time and Mr. Sears came to the rescue, commissioning Grose to build a body upon a Rolls Royce chassis. This was probably secondhand. Nevertheless, it was a generous gift, presented to the Brigade in 1938. At about the same time another ambulance was being built, for use by the S.J.A.B. based at the Margaret Spencer Convalescent Home at Dallington, on a Vauxhall 25hp chassis.

169 *The 'Burcote' was also available on the Adelphi chassis with slightly modified body lines*

170 *Grose estate car body on a 1935 Commer chassis*

171   *Grose estate car body on a 1935 Commer chassis*

172   *Even with the hood raised this Invicta retained it's sporting lines*

173   *A pretty little body built on a 1936 Lanchester Light Six chassis*

In the bus-building world techniques were changing. The traditional metal on wood construction was being questioned and Grose's experimented with a new design for an all-metal coach assembled from panels specially imported from the Wayne company of Detroit in the United States of America. This was an all-weather safety coach built on an English Bedford chassis. By adding sections the body could be constructed in varying sizes from 20- to 40-seaters. Years before its time, the system was later adopted by most firms, but when it was shown at the Commercial Motor Show held at Earls Court it attracted much comment but did not catch on.

Grose's General Motors agency brought the Canadian-built Buick range into the showrooms in the early days of 1938. That year's models boasted what were described as Dynaflash engines, torque-free springing, and streamlined bodies in a typically trans-atlantic bulbous form.

Fifty years had passed since the founding of the firm and the occasion was celebrated by extending the workshops at Pike Lane right through to Horsemarket, increasing the garage service department to no less than four times its existing size. An imposing new entrance from Horsemarket was constructed in modern style. A concrete structure, it had island petrol pumps under cover with a kiosk in the central buttress and customer

174 *Grose's hearse body for a 1937 Vauxhall chassis*

waiting rooms in the left and right ends. Offices also ranged along the first floor. Inside, the garage was tiled to a height of three feet six inches in cream glazed brick, the upper part painted beige. The floor was a patented non-absorbent material. A new heating system was installed, doing away with the old 'Tortoise' stoves that still provided intermittent heat in some of the older areas and were dangerous with the new and most commonly used cellulose paints.

High pressure hoses were installed in washing bays with grill floors. An ingenious system collected water from the vast area of roofing and channelled it down to two 2,000-gallon storage tanks in the basement to use for washing vehicles. To facilitate under-car servicing the old system of 'loose board rabbit warrens' and primitive hoists was dispensed with and two large new grilled-floor inspection pits were made, one accommodating five cars at a time, the other three commercial vehicles. The pits were lined in glazed brick and flanked by workbenches.

With an eye to staff comfort, a new and modern messroom was provided for workers and a large toilet department equipped with hot and cold sprays. This also

175 *Unusually, an Armstrong Siddeley chassis bore Grose hearse coachwork*

was registered as a branch of the Bedford Drivers Club, of which there were over 50,000 members in Great Britain, 300 of them in Northampton and district.

Grose's had, the previous year, inaugurated an insurance scheme and benevolent fund for their employees. Perhaps it was this concern for their craftsmen that resulted in at least 25 of their employees having served 12 years or more at the jubilee; some indeed had notched up 25 or 30 years.

Begun in 1938 and designed by local architect H.J. Ingham, work progressed in the hands of Messrs A.P. Hawtin and Sons until the new garage was opened in March 1939.

About this time, too, Grose's absorbed the premises of the old *Spencer Hotel*, adjacent to their premises in Marefair. In earlier days it had been the residence of Dr. J.M. Bryan.

In Pike Lane Grose's still occupied a small row of terraced cottages, the one nearest the garage entrance lived in by Frank Barratt, caretaker and general factotum, and the next one by Sam Randall, the firm's top mechanic.

176   *A bizarre choice for a Grose hearse body was the little Citroën chassis*

As the clouds of war loomed large over Europe, the future of all companies dealing in luxury items like motor cars looked bleak. More important for the Grose family was the fact that the founder of the firm and doyen of local motorists, Joseph George, was becoming more infirm. In his later years he had taken pleasure in shooting and angling until his eyesight started to fail. He then took up pheasant breeding as a hobby, specialising in the brilliantly coloured foreign species, showing them with considerable success.

In Freemasonry he held the highest positions, twice being the Worshipful Master of the Fidelity Lodge, a member of the Pomfret Lodge, and a founder member of St John's Lodge, Past M.E.Z. of the Northampton Chapter, and Past Provincial Grand Warden of Northants and Hunts.

One of Joseph's little eccentricities was his partiality for the company of tramps. On the advice of his doctor he took to walking some 20 or 30 miles a day. Clad in his oldest suit and a pair of stout boots with his customary green eyeshade pulled low on his brow, he was often taken for a tramp. Indeed he frequently sought out these vagrants and was accepted by them as an equal, becoming something of an expert on their habits and ways. He used to chortle over one of his favourite stories. Apparently four 'gentlemen of the road' were all walking along a road near Daventry chatting amicably when the conversation was rudely interrupted by the hooting of a motor car horn. Startling them into the verge, a large luxurious limousine swept by leaving three of the tramps shaking their fists and hurling abuse after the dissappearing tail of the car. The foursome continued on their way with much discussion about the ways of the

177   *Workmen use an elevating platform by Grose on a 1937 Bedford chassis to put up Coronation decorations in Abington Street, Northampton*

'idle rich' and their chauffeurs. Imagine their surprise when, just around the corner, there was parked the limousine and their companion slid in beside the driver and was driven nonchalantly off. The 'tramp' was none other than Joseph Grose, and the 'chauffeur' Councillor Harvey Reeves who had arranged to pick Grose up on his way back from Leamington.

In later years his walks were restricted to Duston and back. Eventually he became almost totally blind. Joseph George Grose died on 30 December 1939 at his home 'The Limes', Weedon Road.

Son Will took over as managing director with Frank as sales director. Miss Kate Grose was company secretary. Soon after, the company name of the Northampton Motor Omnibus Company, which had been retained, was changed with the approval of the Board of Trade to Northampton Motor Services Limited in order to operate the Daimler, Lanchester, Aston Martin, and Lagonda dealerships.

The Kingsthorpe coachworks were requisitioned by the army during the war and used for servicing half-track personnel carriers and as a store. The craftsmen, those that

178   *A Grose bodied ambulance for St John Ambulance Brigade on a 1939 25hp Vauxhall chassis*

179   *Constructed to an American patent design, Grose showed this Bedford based coach at Earls Court*

180   *Extending the garage through to a new Horsemarket entrance in 1938*

were not called up, were moved down to the Marefair garage where they, too, concentrated on the servicing of army vehicles. As they had in the First World War, Grose's also converted several private cars to serve as ambulances. Interestingly, two brand new Vauxhall chassis stored on joists above the mill in Pike Lane were retrieved to be given ambulance bodies.

Bill Grose went to the Rover company where he did experimental work on the Whittle jet engine. When this programme was transferred to Rolls Royce he moved with it as an engineer assisting with the test flying of engines, remaining there until 1950.

John Grose went to the Alvis works until the factory was bombed and he moved to Rover where he also worked on jet engines. When he went into uniform he served as an engineer with the Fleet Air Arm.

The war was just drawing to an end in 1945 as Grose Ltd. celebrated their 50 years' association with the Rover company. Of course, Joseph's friendship with John Kemp Starley predated 1895 by many years, but this was the official silver jubilee of the alliance of the two firms. To mark the event a dinner was held at the Masonic Hall attended by 90 guests at which a fine model of a 1940 Rover sports saloon, made especially by the Northampton model-makers Bassett-Lowke Ltd., was presented to Mr. S.B. Wilks, the chairman of Rover. It was intended to replace a similar model that had been destroyed in the Coventry blitz of 1941. In return a massive silver inkstand was presented to the Northampton firm.

181   *At St Mary's Street the jumble of units acquired through the decades were swept away for one open construction*

Five

Modern Times

Immediately after the war, echoing the situation in the early '20s, there was a post-war boom in motoring. The Marefair premises had space for over 300 cars at this time, but a planned strategy of expansion was put into place. One of the first moves was the purchase of Headlands Garage Ltd. in Kettering and its change of name to Grose (Kettering) Ltd. Further extension of the Pike Lane premises took place, enlarging the stores and the tyre departments, together with the widening of the showroom into the old *Spencer Hotel* building.

In the aftermath of the war an unusual attraction drew motorists to the Marefair showrooms. In March 1947 the huge bullet-proof Grosse Mercedes, which had been the parade car of Field Marshal Hermann Goering, was put on display. Weighing some five tons, it had been captured by British forces when they overran a Luftwaffe vehicle park in Schleswig-Holstein. A sixpenny admission was charged to view the car and donated to the Soldiers', Sailors' and Airmen's Families Association.

When the annual London to Brighton veteran car run was re-established after the war, Will Grose continued his participation as a keen member of the Veteran Car Club of Great Britain. In 1947 he successfully completed the run in the firm's 1903 Wolseley, a wagonette originally built for the Earl of Berkeley. This he continued to do for many years, although 1953 brought both good and bad news for his participation in the event. That year Will Grose, who had taken part in the run every year since 1937, was laid low with chronic back trouble which prevented him taking part. The good news was that the Veteran Car Club had re-examined the evidence regarding the car's production date and after due deliberation concluded that it was a 1902 model, not 1903. Two years later, in 1955, the car took part in a re-enactment of an historic motoring occasion. On St Patrick's Day in 1909, when the army was still sceptical about the usefulness of motor cars in wartime, the Automobile Association had demonstrated their ability to move infantry about rapidly by carrying a detachment of the Guards from London to Hastings. On 15 March 1955 members of the V.C.C., again carried soldiers to the coast. The Grose Wolseley, with its appropriate plate WL9999, acquitted itself with honour.

Bill Grose, the eldest son of Will, took a keen interest in motor sport and when, in 1948, the new Formula 500 racing started he adopted it with enthusiasm, constructing the Grose 500 powered by a 500cc JAP speedway-type engine. This was the category of car that gave such later stars as Stirling Moss, Peter Collins and John Cooper their start in motor racing.

182 *The Grose 500 race car ready for the International Grand Prix at Silverstone on 2 October 1948, the first big meeting at this now famous circuit.*

On 2 October 1948 the Royal Automobile Club ran the first big post-war race meeting on a derelict wartime bomber airfield at Silverstone. Supporting the International Grand Prix was a race for the new 500cc cars and Bill Grose, with brother John as reserve driver, lined up the Grose car alongside such stars as Moss, Ken Wharton and Spike Rhiando. Two laps into the event and a flying stone cut a brake pipe leaving the car brakeless. A temporary repair allowed it to continue for six more laps before lost fluid caused officials to black flag the Grose.

In the search for more performance a double-knocker Norton engine was fitted, resulting in a spell of modest success. After an 18-month lay-off, Bill Grose came back in May 1953 with a new, smaller and lighter, rear-engined car, but the class was outgrowing it's roots and was soon to disappear. He gave up racing in 1956.

John, meanwhile, also had competition success but in the world of rallying, before turning his energy towards his real love, motorcycle scrambling. He raced both two-stroke Dot and four-stroke BSA Gold Star machines but never won the race that he

183 *In the search for more power a Norton 'double-knocker' engine was fitted for the following season. The car is seen at the 1949 Silverstone Grand Prix meeting.*

184 *John Grose hustles his Dot machine through a bend at the Northampton Motor Cyclists Club scramble at Sywell in April 1954.*

so wanted to win, the famous Wild and Woolly at Blisworth. Now the oldest, and some say the toughest, such event being run, this is an annual mud-plug run each year on Boxing Day by the Northampton Motor Cyclists Club. For three years in succession John finished second but still regrets that he could never achieve the coveted first place.

It was John who discovered the firm's now highly prized vehicle, a 1904 Rover. Appropriately for the firm which was the first official Rover distributor, John Grose had been looking for an early example of the marque for years when, in 1950, he began to hear rumours of an old car mouldering in a shed behind a Cambridgeshire garage. Investigations revealed the veteran Rover serving as a hen roost.

The car was one of the first models offered by the Rover company, a single cylinder, three speed, 8hp vehicle introduced in 1904 with a price tag of £210 that was so popular that it remained in production until 1912. Capable of 30 miles per hour maximum and returning 30 miles per gallon of fuel, when first marketed the model had primitive wire and bobbin steering which was almost immediately dropped in favour of a rack and pinion system. The car John found was of the earliest type.

The original owner is unknown, as is the first registration number, but it came into the possession of a garage at Swavesey in payment of a debt sometime in the 1920s. There it remained until after the Second World War when the garage was taken over by a new owner. His original intention to restore it had to be shelved due to pressure of business and the car was seen to be deteriorating so, after some negotiation, it was sold to John Grose for £25. A nut and bolt restoration revealed a remarkably original car. One extraordinary occurrence during the restoration was when

185 *Mr. and Mrs. W.L. 'Bill' Grose cross the Madeira Drive, Brighton, finishing line in the 1904 Rover car to complete the 1954 Veteran Car Run.*

it was found that the engine's main roller bearings, of a type obsolete by half a century, were found to be unserviceable. Grose's storeman at Northampton amazingly located original spares on the shelf, a legacy of the firm's long association with the makers! The car, meticulously restored and carrying the registration mark BVV2, has completed several London to Brighton runs and now graces J. Grose Ltd.'s East Anglia show-rooms.

Tragedy struck in 1958/59 when all three second generation members of the Grose family working within the business died in a short space of time. Miss Kate, known as Katie, was unmarried, having stayed at home to look after her father, as was commonly the case in days gone by. She had for 30 years served as a director and company secretary of Grose Ltd. Despite this commitment she was a past president of the Soroptimists Club of Northampton and founded the St James's branch of the Women's Voluntary Service.

Brother Frank died suddenly on 18 May 1959, aged 62, at Gorleston. The youngest of Joseph's five children, he had been educated at Northampton Grammar School, had served as an ambulance driver during World War I and with the Royal Engineers. A keen rugger supporter, he was a founder member of the Old Northamptonians R.F.C. and sat on the committee of the Saints. For 20 years he was a Special Constable and did a long spell as group scoutmaster at St James's End. Within the company he had been in charge of the N.M.O.C. operation and lately sales director. He left a widow, a son Gerald, and a daughter Pat.

Then, on 30 November 1959, William Thomas Grose passed away in the Northampton General Hospital. Joseph's eldest son, he was 70 years old. He, too, had been educated at the Grammar School, afterwards serving a six-year apprenticeship at Rover's factories at Coventry and Liverpool. He came back to join the family firm in 1911.

The third generation stepped forward to fill the gaps, with William Lloyd (Bill) as chairman and managing director, Gerald running the Northampton operation and John Stanley at Kettering.

On 29 November 1963 a grand celebration dinner was held at the Salon ballroom in St James's End to mark the firm's 75th birthday. After a sumptuous meal of escalope of Angus fillet Marsala, various other courses, all washed down with best wines and brandy, The Company was toasted by L.G.T. Farmer, chairman of the Rover Company and president of the S.M.M.T. The local press made great play of the innovation of smoking between courses and before the loyal toast that was encouraged at this dinner. On the menu, between the fish and the meat course, was iced sorbet and Russian cigarettes. The idea was to cleanse the palate, but it was the first time that the continental custom had been seen in Northampton.

Almost immediately the name of the company was changed to the now more appropriate Grose Holdings Ltd.; the old buildings at Marefair, Pike Lane, and Horsemarket were sold, and new purpose-built five-acre premises at Queen's Park Parade, Kingsthorpe were commissioned. The move was finally made in May 1965, being achieved in 11 days.

Once the Kingsthorpe premises were up and running the management structure was reorganised with John Grose as chairman. The coachworks lower down the hill, on the site of the original Croft's premises, were sold. By this time they had long ceased to build custom-built bodies on private cars but survived by operating as a separate commercial vehicle depot and paintshop. What remained of this trade was incorporated into the new premises.

The family name of Grose is an unusual one, its origins unknown. A curious connection materialised from an unexpected quarter in June 1966 when two stunt drivers named Peter and Bob Grose of Hollywood, U.S.A., brought their Canadian Hell Drivers show to England. They had just completed a world tour that included Australia, Hong Kong, the Phillipines, Kuwait, Lebanon, and South Africa. The Northampton firm sponsored their performance at Brafield stock car stadium on the strength of the name, although there is no family link as far as is known.

In 1969 Westonia Garage at Weston Favell was acquired from local entrepreneur, Andre Baldet. These premises had an interesting history, starting in 1933 as Northampton's first all-electric garage and filling station. It passed through several hands before joining the Grose empire under a seperate company title, Grose Westonia Ltd. The franchises for Daimler, Jaguar, Rover, Rolls Royce, and Bentley were moved to here and the Triumph agency was added to the Kingsthorpe operation. This reorganisation was carried out in an endeavour to comply with the British Leyland Motor Corporation's exclusivity of distribution policy. B.L.M.C., however, felt that the moves were not sufficient to meet their requirements and threatened to disfranchise the company from 1 January 1974. It was decided, therefore, to dispose of Grose Westonia Ltd. and the sale was completed on 2 April 1973, to Thomas Barlow (Holdings) Ltd.

When in April 1973 new county authorities were set up in a national reorganisation John Grose stood for election as Conservative candidate for Castle Ashby, the area he had already represented on the County Council since 1970.

Not far away from Grose's new Queens Park premises was Bective Garage Ltd. which had been founded by Horace Gibbes, a Grose apprentice. In 1978 he took the decision to retire. Grose Ltd. bought the company and re-organised it as Grose Eurocars.

A significant step was the take-over, in June 1975, of the long established firm of H.E. Nunn Ltd. of Ipswich, then being operated by Mann Egerton Ltd., to become Grose Ipswich Ltd. The next stage came in September 1980 when Grose Holdings Ltd. was split for administrative reasons. Bill Grose took control of the Northampton portion with Bedford and Vauxhall agencies, similar outlets, together with Fiat and Volvo, at Swinn and Marlborough, a filling station at Collingtree, and premises at Kettering, while John established John Grose Group Limited, based on the Ipswich company, and operated the Volkswagen Audi service station at Newport Pagnell together with a lease hire establishment from a head office at Wellingborough. The name John Grose Group Ltd. was chosen as it followed the initials of Joseph George Grose, the founder of the firm.

John Grose Group Ltd. placed its full weight behind that of the Ford Motor Company with the declared intention of remaining exclusively Ford dealers. In 1981 the Ford car and truck main dealership at Lowestoft, Days Garage Ltd., was acquired and the headquarters were moved from Wellingborough to Lowestoft.

In 1989 the most significant move took place when John Grose Ltd. acquired a $5\frac{1}{2}$-acre freehold site on the burgeoning Ransomes Europark, on the northern side of Ipswich. Opened in May 1990, it was a new concept in car sales and servicing. Light and airy modern buildings in a park-style setting included such features as a coffee shop, safe undercover children's play area, and observation deck, where mum and the kids can be comfortable while dad browses or waits for the car to be dealt with. This development was the largest single investment made in the history of the company and was granted 'Pilot Dealer' status by the Ford Motor Company.

At this time, though, the recession was having a devastating effect on the commercial vehicle industry and Grose's Ford Truck Specialist Dealer premises at Hadleigh Road in Ipswich was feeling the pinch. In November 1991 the decision was made to reduce the firm's involvement in trucks to concentrate on cars. To this end the two-acre site at Hadleigh Road, which the company had occupied for 13 years, was sold.

Since that time John Grose Group Ltd. has also absorbed the Lynford Motor Company Ltd. of Kings Lynn and expanded its Ford dealership into Woodbridge and

Wisbech. In November 1996 the Ford main dealer trading as Mereside Ford at Diss, in Norfolk, was acquired.

In February 1996 the decision was made to dispose of the Kettering operation and W. Grose Ltd. sold it to the Corby Vauxhall dealers Forest Gate.

Over a century has passed since the founding of the firm and Joseph Grose would be astonished to know that the companies that have developed from that little shop in St James's End are two of the largest provincial distributors of motorcars in the country. In 1997 W. Grose Ltd. operated five Vauxhall outlets and one Fiat, employing 240 staff and turning over £50m a year. That same year the John Grose Group, an all-Ford operation based at Lowestoft, had seven outlets throughout East Anglia with 370 employees and an annual turnover of £80m.

Joseph Grose lived to see the motor car develop from a rich man's toy to everyman's neccessity. Sadly, he also saw individuality expressed in craftsman-built bespoke carriagework disappear in favour of off-the-peg uniformity. Just a few examples of classic Grose bodywork survive and he would, I'm sure, be delighted to see the way that his work is appreciated and cherished by today's enthusiasts.

Appendices

The following appendices list what is known about chassis, both private and commercial, upon which Grose bodies were constructed. Unfortunately, all company records of chassis numbers, body types, delivery dates, and customers, have been lost or destroyed over the years during moves and developments. What survives has been assembled, or deduced, from the remaining scraps of information supplied by dedicated enthusiasts for individual marques and vehicle types.

Appendix I

RENAULT	Supplied 1913		
January	13.9hp	inclined chassis	No.114
	13.9hp	C4 complete	No.216
	15.8hp	C4 complete	No.238
February	26.9hp	chassis	No.371
	13.9hp	C4 complete	No.317
March	13.9hp	C4 complete	No.414
	15.8hp	C4 complete	No.445
	15.8hp	C4 complete	No.450

Complete cars supplied with four-seater body, hood, screen, scuttle-dash, side doors, five lamps and horn, all of standard type.

Appendix II

Talbot vehicles delivered to Grose Ltd. for bodying by them

Chassis No.	Ordered	Body type	Purchased by	Model
2991	29/7/30	1930 Motor Show car		AO90 (9ft. 3in.)
32815	5/8/31	1931 Motor Show car Close coupled coupé	Warwick Wright	AM90 (10ft.)
35006	17/8/32	Four-seater coupé	Glovers of Ripon	AV95
35060	12/12/32	Sports coupé	Motor Mac's	AV95
33721	29/1/33	Touring	H.C. Hutchinson	AW75
34133	30/6/33	Touring	L.E. Taylor	AW75
34416	1/10/34	Touring	Lewis Bros	AW75
35657	11/5/34	1933 Motor Show car Continental coupé	Pass & Joyce	AV95
35658	2/5/34	Continental coupé	Pass & Joyce	AV95
35659	11/5/34	Continental coupé	Pass & Joyce	AV95

Additional to these Grose bodied cars, the company also purchased many Talbot cars with Darracq bodies. This list is incomplete, relating only to 1930 to 1936.

Chassis type	Quantity	Chassis type	Quantity
AO75 sports	3	AW75 (Long)	9
AM75	3	BA75	1
AQ14/45	6	AV95	3
AU65	2	BD75	1
AX65	9	BI105	2
AW75	3	BD105	3

Appendix III

Grose bus bodies supplied to local operators

Mark	Make	Type	Chassis No.	Type of body	Seats	Remarks
YORK BROS 'EASY' COACHES						
RP2051	Chevrolet		R7070T	Bus	14	New January 1926
NV2049	Maudslay	ML4ES	4932	Normal control	26	New January 1933. Rebodied as 20-seater by Grose in June 1934 for long distance work. Replaced with Burlingham body September 1937.
NV3493	Maudslay	ML3H	5111	Forward control	32	Shown at Olympia Motor Show March 1934. Rear entrance.
NV5812	Dodge	PLB	1058		20	New August 1935
VV3698	Maudslay	SF40	5209	Streamlined	32	New April 1935. Renovated 1938 with modified front.
VV3834	Maudslay	SF40	5230	Streamlined	32	New March 1935. Renovated 1938 with modified front.
LAWS OF BRAFIELD						
NV611	Bedford	WLB	108028	Bus	20	Sold to York's August 1935. Body later fitted to NV5812.
STAN SMITH OF IRTHLINGBOROUGH						
NV3605	Leyland	Cub	Forward control			Sold to United Counties May 1938.
ARTHUR BASFORD OF GREENS NORTON						
NV9386	Albion	Victor	25016E		31	New June 1937. Renovated by Grose 1947 with modified front.
PHILLIPS OF LONG BUCKBY						
RY6495	Chevrolet	LO	40293	Front entrance	12	New 1928. Sold to United Counties July 1932.
ABBOTTS OF GREAT DODDINGTON						
RP8163	G.M.C.			Bus		

Appendix IV

Grose bodied buses supplied to Northampton Corporation Tramways

Year	Reg. No.	Make	Type	Grose body type	Decommissioned	Remarks
GROSE BODIED BUSES SUPPLIED TO NORTHAMPTON CORPORATION TRAMWAYS.						
1927	NH7632	Guy	B	B26F	1940	
1927	NH7633	Guy	B	B26F	1940	
1927	NH7634	Guy	B	B26F	1940	Ended as Dick's Snack Bar, Abergavenny, 1948
1927	NH7635	Guy	B	B26F	1940	
1928	NH8496	Guy	FCX	B32D	1947	
1929	NH8994	Guy	FCX	H28/26R	1939	
1929	NH8995	Guy	FCX	H28/26R	1939	Fitted with Crossley diesel 1934
1929	NH8996	Guy	FCX	H28/26R	1941	
1929	NH8997	Guy	FCX	H28/26R	1943	
1929	NH8998	Guy	FCX	H28/26R	1943	
1929	NH9189	Guy	FCX	H28/26R	1939	
1929	NH9190	Guy	FCX	H28/26R	1939	
1929	NH9191	Guy	FCX	H28/26R	1943	
1929	NH9315	Guy	FCX	H28/26R	1944	
1929	NH9316	Guy	FCX	H28/26R	1944	
1930	NH9704	Guy	FCX	H28/26R	1943	
1930	VV117	Guy	FCX	H28/26R	1944	Fitted with Crossley diesel 1935
1930	VV118	Guy	FCX	H28/26R	1944	Fitted with Crossley diesel 1935
1930	VV119	A.E.C.	Renown	H28/26R	1945	Bus No.40
1930	VV160	Guy	FCX	H28/26R	1945	Fitted with Crossley diesel 1935
1930	VV161	Guy	FCX	H28/26R	1945	Fitted with Crossley diesel 1935
1930	VV162	Guy	FCX	H28/26R	1945	
GROSE BODIED BUSES SUPPLIED TO NORTHAMPTON CORPORATION TRANSPORT						
1932	VV1161	Dennis	Lancet	B26F	1944	
1932	VV1162	Dennis	Lancet	B26F	1944	
1932	VV1163	Dennis	Lancet	B26F	1948	
1932	VV1164	Dennis	Lancet	B26F	1950	
1932	VV1165	Dennis	Lancet	B26F	1944	
1932	VV1166	Dennis	Lancet	B26F	1951	
1932	VV1167	Dennis	Lancet	B26F	1951	
1932	VV1168	Dennis	Lancet	B26F	1951	

Appendix V

Vehicles taken over from Northampton Motor Omnibus Co. by United Counties Omnibus Co. in 1928

Mark	Make	Type	Chassis No.	Type of body	Seats	Tyres	Licensed	Remarks
NH2571	Daimler	B		Double decker	32	Solid	no	
BD2829	Daimler	W		Double decker	32	Solid	no	Body off chassis. Chassis dismantled
NH1693	Daimler	W		Double decker	32	Solid	Yes	
NH1857	Clyde	OB		Charabanc	32	Solid	No	
NH1694	Daimler	B		Double decker	32	Solid	No	
BD2484	Daimler	W		Double decker	32	Solid	No	
NH2517	Daimler	W		Double decker	32	Solid	Yes	
NH2719	Daimler	W		Double decker	32	Solid	No	
NH2928	Daimler	W		Double decker	32	Solid	No	
NH4092	Daimler	B		Saloon	32	Pneumatic	Yes	Billington body
NH4091	Daimler	Y		Double decker	32	Solid	Yes	
NH6506	Chevrolet	T		Saloon	14	Pneumatic	Yes	Grose body
NH2720	Daimler	B		Saloon	32	Solid	Yes	Cremmon body
NH2853	Daimler	CD		Charabanc	32	Solid	No	
NH6419	Chevrolet	T		Saloon	14	Pneumatic	Yes	London Lorries body
NH6667	Chevrolet	T		Saloon	14	Pneumatic	Yes	London Lorries body
NH6589	Chevrolet	T		Saloon	14	Pneumatic	Yes	London Lorries body
NH4249	Daimler	Y		Double decker	32	Solid	Yes	
NH4248	Daimler	B		Double decker	32	Solid	No	
NH4447	Daimler	Y		Double decker	32	Solid	No	
NH4519	Daimler	Y		Double decker	32	Solid	Yes	
XB9885	Daimler	B		Saloon	40	Solid	Yes	Strachan & Brown body 5-ton chassis
NH4819	Daimler	Y	1815	Saloon	40	Pneumatic	Yes	Strachan & Brown body New 1923
XB8005	Daimler	Y		Double decker	32	Solid	No	Engine out of chassis
NH5042	Daimler	Y		Saloon	32	Solid	No	Billington body
NH5423	Daimler	Y	Y5328	Saloon	40	Pneumatic	Yes	Strachan & Brown body New March 1924
NH5618	Daimler	Y	Y4544	Saloon	40	Pneumatic	Yes	Strachan & Brown body New 1924
NH5315	Vulcan	2T		Saloon	26	Pneumatic	Yes	Strachan & Brown body
NH3172	Daimler	CB		Saloon	26	Pneumatic	Yes	Strachan & Brown body
NH6327	Daimler	Y	3377	Saloon	32	Pneumatic	Yes	Grose body. New June 1925
XF9423	Daimler	Y	Y25306	Saloon	32	Pneumatic	Yes	Grose body
NH6507	Graham			Saloon	20	Pneumatic	Yes	Grose body
XK7356	Daimler	CB		Saloon	26	Pneumatic	Yes	Grose body

Index

HALF-WAY HOUSE,

KINGSTHORPE ROAD, NORTHAMPTON.

PROPRIETOR ... ... R. C. TOOBY.

ONE MILE OPEN
BICYCLE HANDICAP,
SATURDAY, JANUARY 12th, 1878,

First Prize, £3; Second, £1 5s.; Third, 10s.
Fourth, 5s.

HEAT 1.		HEAT 5.	
1 G. Keynes	192	1 J. Wildman	155
2 H. Luck	170	2 W. Tyrrell	125
3 F. Frewin	150	3 W. Favell	22
4 F. Allen	130	4 T. Rigby	142
HEAT 2.		HEAT 6.	
1 E. Fascutt	175	1 P. Gross	220
2 Herbert Walker	205	2 E. Webb	170
3 Church's Novice	160	3 W. Heap	185
4 T. Leeson	90	4 R. Pinkard	22
HEAT 3.		HEAT 7.	
1 M. Whiting, Well.	100	1 J. Gross	210
2 H. Coleman	170	2 A. Ward	180
3 W. Shrubsole	150	3 J. Whitehouse	170
4 W. Church	155	4 C. Tompkins	22
HEAT 4.		HEAT 8.	
1 W. Hamsley	160	1 S. Braines	70
2 A. Starmer	170	2 G. Webb	175
3 E. Bingham	165	3 T. Wood	205
4 T. Norris	175	4 F. Farrer, Kettering	95
		5 J. Leeson	180

HEAT 9.		HEAT 11.	
1 W. Law	170	1 G. Nobles	155
2 W. Brown	240	2 H. Smith	100
3 J. Connoly	165	3 A. Tomkins	170
4 C. Baucutt	168	4 A. Hawker	170
HEAT 10.		HEAT 12.	
1 F. Miller	195	1 H. Linnett	162
2 T. Favell	195	2 C. Starmer	220
3 W. Sadd	165	3 G. Edlin, Leicester	0
4 J. Osborn	165	4 W. Wilson	40
5 E. Westley	195		

Each Competitor to start from Stool or Chair, no attendant allowed to touch the Machine.

Competitors allowed to use any machine they please.

FINALS RUN ON SATURDAY, JAN. 19

FIRST HEAT EACH DAY AT 1.30 PROMPT.

ADMISSION 3D.

NOTICE.— Mr. COLLIER'S 200 YARDS HANDICAP will take place on SATURDAY and MONDAY, January 26 & 28, 1878.

Parker, Printer, Newland, Northampton.

1888 - 1963

75th
Anniversary Luncheon

GROSE Limited
29th November 1963

The Salon, Franklins Gardens, Northampton